THE UBUNTU BEGINNER'S GUIDE - TWELFTH EDITION

JONATHAN MOELLER

DESCRIPTION

Description

The Ubuntu Beginner's Guide (Twelfth Edition) gives users new to Ubuntu Linux an overview of the operating system, from simple command-line tasks to advanced server configuration.

In the Guide, you'll learn how to:

-Use the Ubuntu command line.

-Manage users, groups, and file permissions.

-Install software on a Ubuntu system, both from the command line, the GUI, and using the Snappy application management system.

-Configure network settings.

-Use the vi editor to edit system configuration files.

-Install and configure a Samba server for file sharing.

-Install SSH for remote system control using public key/private key encryption.

-Install a LAMP server.

-Install web applications like WordPress and Drupal.

-Configure an FTP server.

-Manage ebooks.

-Convert digital media.

-Manage and configure GNOME Shell, the new default Ubuntu environment.

-Manage and configure Unity, the old default Ubuntu environment.

-Manage and halt processes from the command line.

-Set up both a VNC server and a client

-And many other topics.

LEGAL INFORMATION

The Ubuntu Beginner's Guide - Twelfth Edition
Jonathan Moeller
Copyright 2011 by Jonathan Moeller.
Originally published in ebook format May 2011.
Second edition ebook format published August 2011.
Third edition ebook format published January 2012.
Fourth edition ebook format published July 2012.
Fifth edition ebook format published December 2012.
Sixth edition ebook format published August 2013.
Seventh edition ebook format published April 2014.
Eighth edition ebook format published November 2016.
Ninth edition ebook format published June 2017.
Tenth edition ebook format published November 2017.
Eleventh edition ebook format published May 2018.
Twelfth edition ebook format published February 2019.
Cover image copyright Andresr Imaging | istockphoto.com

INTRODUCTION - WELCOME TO UBUNTU

Welcome to the eleventh edition of "The Ubuntu Beginner's Guide!" If you're reading this book, you have the opportunity to learn more about Ubuntu, one of the most powerful and useful modern operating systems. Ubuntu is extremely versatile – it can be configured to perform almost any computing task. New users can use Ubuntu as a simple machine for web surfing, social networking, and email. Advanced users can perform a range of tasks from document preparation to image editing and software development, and gamers can play a variety of entertaining games on Ubuntu. Network administrators can configure Ubuntu to perform almost any server task – from a file-sharing server to a host for a web application (like WordPress or Drupal) to a DHCP server.

Ubuntu also benefits from low system requirements, and can often run on older machines that are unable to handle Windows 7 or Windows 10. Ubuntu only requires a 2 gigahertz processor, 2 gigabytes of RAM, and 25 gigabytes of hard drive space – and there are variants, like Xubuntu, that require even less, and can run on even older machines. The Server Edition of Ubuntu requires only a 300 megahertz processor, 256 megabytes of RAM, and 1.5 gigabytes of hard drive space, allowing you to get more useful life out of old machines.

Ubuntu also has the advantage of immunity to the many forms of malware that plague Windows-based systems. No operating system is perfectly safe, of course, but fewer varieties of viruses and Trojans will run on Ubuntu.

Finally, Ubuntu gives you access to a vast array of software, most of it free, that will help you accomplish whatever task you choose.

What Is Ubuntu?

What exactly is "Ubuntu", though? Technically, the full name of the current long-term support version as of this writing is "Ubuntu Linux 18.04 Bionic Beaver." But what exactly does that mean?

"Linux" refers generally to a family of free operating systems based upon the Linux kernel (a kernel is the core component of any operating system). The history of Linux is long and complex, but we can provide a brief sketch here. In the late 1960s and 1970s, AT&T's Bell Labs developed the UNIX operating system, which was soon used in university computer labs across the United States.

However, AT&T retained the rights to the UNIX code, which meant that people could not freely alter or distribute it. In response to this, computer programmer Richard Stallman launched the GNU Project in 1983. (GNU stands for "GNU's Not Unix.") Stallman's goal with the GNU Project was to create a UNIX-like operating system that was nonetheless free to alter and distribute under the principle of "Free Software", a philosophical position which argued that software should be free to distribute and alter without legal restrictions. The GNU Project and Stallman himself produced a large number of software tools and programs. Unfortunately, the GNU Project lacked a viable kernel, the necessary core of any operating system.

This changed in 1991 when a Finnish university student named Linus Torvald became frustrated with the academic licensing for Minix, a UNIX-like operating system restricted to educational use. Torvalds wrote his own kernel, named it Linux, and released it under the GNU free license. Combined with the GNU project, the Linux kernel provided a freely available operating system – an operating system that people could modify and distribute however they saw fit.

Linux had been born.

(Many people insist that the proper name of Linux should in fact be GNU\Linux, in recognition of GNU's vital role, and many GNU programs are used in Linux to this day.)

Under the terms of GNU's General Public License (GPL), anyone could modify and distribute Linux. Today, Linux and Linux variants run on every different computing platform, from smartphones to desktop computers to high-end server systems. (Even Amazon's Kindle and Barnes & Noble's Nook e-reader devices are powered by custom versions of Android, a version of Linux designed for smart-phones and tablets.) These different flavors of Linux are called Linux "distributions." Some distributions are commercially supported endeavors, like Red Hat Linux or SuSE Linux, while others are free and community-supported, like Knoppix or Fedora.

One of the more venerable distributions is Debian, started in 1993 by a German programmer named Ian Murdock. Debian is well-known for its stability and its strong devotion to free software principles. Unfortunately, Debian also has a famously slow release cycle. Because of this, Debian is frequently "forked" – a "fork" is when the code of an open-source project (which is free to share and distribute) is used as the foundation for another open-source project.

Ubuntu began as one of these forks. Started by South African entrepreneur Mark Shuttleworth through his company Canonical, Ubuntu focused on providing a smooth experience for the end users, offering a version of Linux for people with little experience with Linux or even with computers in general. Ubuntu issues new releases every six months, accompanied by an alliterative code name: "Hoary Hedgehog", "Breezy Badger", and so on. Each Ubuntu release is supported for 18 months, and every two years a Long-Term Support (LTS) release comes out, which is supported for three years on the desktop version and five years on the server.

Since the releases come out every six months, there's sometimes not much of a noticeable difference between them – the end user would notice very little difference between, say, 10.04 and 10.10. In aggregate, however, the improvements add up – Ubuntu 18.04 Bionic Beaver is a vastly superior operating system over 5.10 Breezy Badger.

Today, Ubuntu is one of the most popular available Linux distributions, with a growing market share and a dedicated community of users and developers.

The Purpose Of This Book

The purpose of this book is to provide a basic introduction to using Ubuntu to perform common tasks. It's not intended as an exhaustive, comprehensive overview, but an introduction to the topic - enough to get you started. (Feel free to jump around if a particular topic interests you more than the others.) I chose the content based upon the most popular posts at my technology blog, Help Desk Screeds, over a year or so. We can divide the book into three rough parts.

-Part I – Using the command line and basic system administration.

-Part II – Using Ubuntu as a server.

-Part III – Games, Wine, and miscellaneous.

We'll also focus on using the command line over the graphical user interface (GUI) whenever possible. Why? For one thing, the Server Edition of Ubuntu does not include a graphical interface. If you want to set up a copy of Ubuntu Server as, say, a web host, you'll need to know how to use the command line. Second, the GUI can sometimes fail. If it does, you'll need knowledge of the command line to restart your system. Third, knowledge of the command line carries over to other Linux distributions, since many other distributions, especially the Debian-based ones, use the same commands as Ubuntu. Knowledge of the Linux command line will even serve you well in Mac OS X. OS X is a version of UNIX, which means that it is a cousin to Linux, and that many of the common Linux commands work in Mac OS X as well (though with some variations).

For a book dedicated solely to using the graphical interface in Ubuntu, check out my The Ubuntu Desktop Beginner's Guide.

Why I Wrote This Book

I used to maintain a technology blog, Help Desk Screeds, at http://www.jonathanmoeller.com/screed, (since retired, and now moved to http://www.computerbeginnersguides.com) and my most popular posts are invariably about Ubuntu. I decided to expand upon some of those posts, write some additional material, and publish it as an ebook. The posts on my blog have helped some people with their Ubuntu questions, and it is my hope that this book will do the same.

Why I started writing about Ubuntu is an interesting story. (Feel free to skip ahead to Chapter 1 if you have no interest in hearing it.) I started using Ubuntu in 2006 with 5.10 Breezy Badger, upgrading with every new release. Meanwhile, I had some success as a writer of fantasy fiction. My sword-and-sorcery novel "Demonsouled" (now available for free at all major online eBook stores) came out from Gale/Five Star in 2005. Like any good writer, I had a blog where I promoted my work and rambled about any fool thing that popped into my head, and like most such blogs, it had virtually zero traffic – I was lucky to get seventy hits in a month.

In April of 2008, Ubuntu 8.04 Dapper Drake came out, and when I upgraded from 7.10, it broke my installation of the Samba file server. I happened to write about this in passing on my blog. To my very great surprise, the post received 60 hits in a single day. Evidently a few other people were having trouble with Samba as well. Surprised, I began writing more and more about Ubuntu, and soon had switched the blog entirely over to technology topics. I sometimes write about Microsoft Windows, Mac OS X, and computer games, but posts about Ubuntu far and away get the most traffic, and so I tend to write about Ubuntu most of the time.

Writing about Ubuntu has been a rewarding experience (and, thanks to Google Adsense and these books, a profitable one as well), and I hope that this book will be useful to you.

Errata

I have done my best to make sure all the information in this book is accurate and timely, and tested every command and procedure described in the following chapters. However, I am only mortal, and undoubtedly I have made mistakes. If you notice any errors, you can email me at jmcontact @ jonathanmoeller.com to let me know. The advantage of ebooks over paper books is that ebooks are vastly easier to update and revise, and I can quickly introduce a revised and updated edition to correct any mistakes. (Another advantage of an ebook is that you can have it open on your computer screen as you work, rather than having to look down at a paper book on your desk.)

Notes On The Second Edition

The first edition of this book came out in May of 2011. Since then, it has sold well enough to merit a second edition. I have added three additional chapters. Chapter 19 discusses managing ebooks on a Ubuntu system. Chapter 20 describes how to convert digital media into different file formats. Chapter 21 describes Unity, the new graphical interface in Ubuntu 11.04 Natty Narwhal (and future editions of Ubuntu), and how to adjust some of its settings.

Notes On The Third Edition

This book continues to sell well enough to merit a third edition - thank you, all! For the third edition, I have added a chapter describing how to manage processes from the command line (Chapter 22). I have also added screenshots for some of the more complex commands.

Notes On The Fourth Edition

This book has sold well enough to make a fourth edition viable - thank you, everyone! Most of the operations described in this book did not change very much in the upgrade from Ubuntu 11.10 Oneiric Ocelot to Ubuntu 12.04 Precise Pangolin, but all chapters have been updated to reflect Precise Pangolin. Additionally, a section on using key-based login for SSH has been added to Chapter 11.

Notes On The Fifth Edition

To my surprise and delight, this book continues to sell. Thank you, all! Combined with the release of Ubuntu 12.10 Quantal Quetzal, that has made it necessary to release an updated fifth edition. Most of the procedures described in this book did not change from Ubuntu 12.04 to Ubuntu 12.10, but I have updated them where necessary. Additionally, I have added a chapter describing how to work with documents such as PDF files from the command line.

Notes On The Sixth Edition

In the sixth edition, we have added a chapter on Ubuntu's built in VNC server and client software.

Notes On The Seventh Edition

The book continues to sell well - thank you, everyone! In the seventh edition we have added installation guides for GLPI and Moodle to the Web Applications chapter, a section on the Unity Tweak Tool utility to the chapter on Unity, and additional information to static DNS settings in the Network chapter.

Notes On The Eighth Edition

After a hiatus of two years, I am pleased to release an eighth edition of this book, updated for Ubuntu 16.04 Xenial Xerus and Ubuntu 16.10 Yakkety Yak. Additionally, Chapter 16: Gaming has been expanded.

Notes On The Ninth Edition

For the ninth edition, we have updated the book for Ubuntu 17.04 Zesty Zapus, and expanded the chapters on networking, installing applications, and gaming.

Notes On The Tenth Edition

The main change for the tenth edition has been an addition of a chapter discussing GNOME Shell, which is now the default Ubuntu desktop environment as of Ubuntu 17.10 Artful Aardvark. The other chapters have been updated as necessary.

Notes On The Eleventh Edition

For the eleventh edition, we have updated the book for Ubuntu 18.04 Bionic Beaver and expanded the sections on GNOME Shell.

Notes On The Twelfth Edition

For the twelfth edition, we have made only a few minor changes to update the book through Ubuntu 18.10 Cosmic Cuttlefish.

INTRODUCTION TO THE COMMAND LINE

WHAT IS THE COMMAND LINE?

The "command line" is shorthand way of saying the "command line interface", also commonly known as the "command prompt" or the "terminal." The command line is a text-based interface. Most people who have used a computer in the last twenty years are accustomed to a graphical interface, whether the various incarnations of Microsoft Windows or Mac OS. A graphical interface has windows, a mouse pointer, a scroll bar, icons, and other graphical representations of files and computer functions. A text-based interface, as the name suggests, has no graphics and relies entirely upon text. You type your commands into the command prompt, which usually looks something like this:

jon@ubuntumachine:~$

Ubuntu then processes your commands and then returns with the results or, if you made a typographical mistake, an error message.

Why use the command line when Ubuntu comes with a highly functional GUI in the new Unity desktop? For one thing, if you want to run Ubuntu as a server, you'll need to know the command line, since the Server Edition of Ubuntu does not come with a GUI. For another reason, many tasks are vastly more efficient from the command line.

Let's say, for example, that you want to copy some JPEG files from your Pictures folder to an external hard drive called BACKUP. More specifically, let's say you want to copy only those JPEG files that have the word "Jamie" in their name to the BACKUP drive. You could open up Pictures folder and drag every "Jamie" JPEG to the BACKUP drive one by one. Or you could open up a Terminal window and type this command:

cp ~/Pictures/*Jamie*.jpg /media/BACKUP

Hit Enter, and the command does all the work for you. No muss, no fuss.

Case Sensitivity

Before we dig into the command line, we need to stress an important point.

All commands and filenames in Linux are case-sensitive!

This can really confuse people coming over from a Windows/DOS background, since neither the old DOS operating system nor the Windows command line were case-sensitive. In other words, Windows would view the files Book.doc, book.doc, and BOOK.doc as the same file. Linux, however, will recognize those as three different files.

In the same way, Linux commands are case sensitive. In Windows/DOS, typing dir, Dir, and DIR into the command prompt will trigger the same **dir** command, which gives a listening of files in the current directory. Linux commands are case-sensitive – ls, Ls, and LS are not the same thing.

Bear this in mind while using the command line.

Filenames With Spaces

The command line does not handle spaces well - say you tried to use the following command to delete a file named "Bob's Term Paper."

rm Bob's Term Paper

This command would fail because the command line would

interpret each word in the command as a separate file. To force the command line to view the file properly, enclose any filename with spaces within quotation marks:

rm "Bob's Term Paper"

This time rm will delete the file.

How To Access The Command Line

If you've never used the command line in Ubuntu before, you might not know how to access it. Fortunately, it's quite simple. There are three ways to launch the command line.

The first way is to go to the Dash (the Ubuntu icon on the upper-left hand corner on your screen, on top of the Launcher) then to click on the Terminal icon. This will launch the GNOME Terminal emulator application, which lets you launch commands from within the GUI.

The second way is to hit the CTRL-ALT-T keys simultaneously, which will immediately open a new Terminal window.

The third way is to hit the CTRL-ALT-F1 keys on your keyboard. Do this, and the GUI will disappear, replaced by a black screen with a logon prompt in white text. Don't be alarmed! This is a "virtual console", which lets you shift the GUI to the background and log in again in a command-line only mode. Your logon session with the GUI will be unaffected – Ubuntu Linux allows multiple logons from the same user at the same time.

You can return to the GUI at any time by hitting CTRL-ALT-F7.

Note that Ubuntu Linux allows you to have seven virtual consoles, from F1 to F7. F7 is reserved for the GUI, and the remaining six allow you to log on using the command line.

The Command Prompt Itself

The command prompt itself, as we've mentioned, will probably look something like this:

jon@ubuntumachine:~$

But what does that mean? Let's break it down.

The "jon", the part before the @ symbol, is the name of the user currently logged into the system. If I am logged into my Ubuntu machine as "jon", then that's the username I'll see before the @ symbol.

The "ubuntumachine", the part after the @ symbol, is the hostname, or the name of the computer. So if my Ubuntu machine is named "ubuntumachine", then that's the hostname you'll see in the command prompt.

The colon (:) marks the division between the part of the prompt that identifies the user and the machine - jon@ubuntumachine - and the part of the prompt that displays the current working directory, which we'll explain below.

The ~ mark refers to the current working directory – in other words, the folder you are currently occupying. (The terms "directory" and "folder" are used interchangeably, though "directory" is used more often in the context of the command line.) In Linux and UNIX, the tilde symbol "~" is shorthand for the user's home directory. So, if I am logged into ubuntumachine as jon, then the ~ is shorthand for the **/home/jon** directory.

This means that if you change your working directory, the command prompt changes as well. Let us say that you change your working directory to /, which in Linux is the root directory. The command prompt will then look like this:

jon@ubuntumachine:/$

Or if you change the working directory to /etc/hp, the prompt will look like this:

jon@ubuntumachine:/etc/hp$

Let's take a look at some useful basic commands.

Finding The Working Directory

The "working directory" refers to the directory where the command prompt is currently focused. As we mention above, the working directory is shown in the command prompt. However, some Linux configurations do not include the working directory in the command prompt by default. To find the working directory, use this command:

pwd

If you're in your Documents folder (a subfolder of your home directory), the output will look something like this:

/home/jon/Documents

Next, let's discuss moving about the Ubuntu filesystem.

Moving From Directory To Directory

You can use the cd command to move from directory to directory from the command line. If you wanted to go to your home directory, for example:

cd ~

To change to the root directory:

cd /

To fully utilize the cd command (and some of the other commands discussed below) you'll need to understand the concept of file paths in Ubuntu Linux.

A "file path" refers to a file's location within the filesystem. Let's say you have a document file named Book.doc stored in your Documents folder. So its absolute location, its exact place in the filesystem, would be this:

/home/jon/Documents/Book.doc

So if you wanted to move to /home/jon/Documents from anywhere in the filesystem, you would use this command:

cd /home/jon/Documents

However, you don't need to type the full path for directories that are subdirectories of the current working directory. If you're already in your home directory, you don't need to type the full path to change to Documents, since Documents is a subdirectory of your home directory. Simply type this:

cd Documents

You can use a similar shortcut to return to the previous directory:

cd ..

The cd command followed by a space and two periods will return you to the next directory up, from Documents to your home folder. Nor does this work only in your home folder – you can use **cd ..** anywhere in the filesystem, and it will move you to your current directory's parent directory.

Of course, once you're inside the directories, you'll actually want to view their contents.

Listing The Contents Of Directories

To view the contents of a directory, use the ls command:

ls

If you use **ls** in your home directory, the output will probably look something like this:

By default, **ls** lists the contents of the current working directory. If you want to view the contents of a different directory, you can either navigate there via the **cd** command, or type the absolute path with the **ls** command. For instance, to view the full contents of the /etc directory:

ls /etc

Pretty simple, right? But the **ls** command doesn't offer very much information. This is a good place to bring up the idea of command options, also known as command switches.

In the context of Linux commands, an "option" is a modifier to a command. It tells the command to perform a slightly different function, or to alter the output somewhat. Run the **ls –l** command in your home directory, and look at how the output changes:

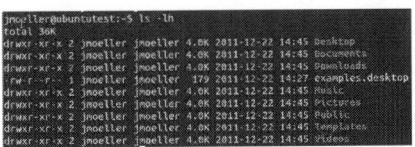

The "l" option stands for "long listing", and ls then shows much more information it does without the option, including the permissions and ownership of the file (we'll discuss those more in the next chapter), along with the file's size and timestamp.

The **ls -l** command is even more useful when combined with the -h option:

You can see how the size of the files are now listened in kilobytes and megabytes, which is often easier to read than just bytes.

YOU CAN ALSO USE the **ls** command with the -a switch to view hidden files:

ls –a

Note all the hidden files in your home directory:

(Most of these hidden files are configuration settings for your account, and should be left alone unless you have a good reason to alter them.)

In Linux, files are hidden by placing a "." in front of their name.

You can hide files yourself by using the **mv** command, which we'll discuss in the next section.

Moving And Renaming Files

To rename a file, you can use the **mv** command. Let's say you wanted to rename the Book.doc file in the current working directory to Roughdraft.doc:

> **mv Book.doc Roughdraft.doc**

The **mv** command will then rename the Book.doc file to Roughdraft.doc.

The mv command can also (as the name suggests) move files from one location to another on your system. If you wanted to move Book.doc from your Documents folder to another folder called Backup in your home directory, you would use the **mv** command like this:

> **mv ~/Documents/Book.doc ~/Backup**

The mv command also works with "wildcards", which are characters that can represent file names. Think of them as variables – you can use them to tell the **mv** command to move "every file that ends with .doc in my Documents folder to the Backup folder." It works like this:

> **mv ~/Documents/*.doc ~/Backup**

This will move every single file with the .doc extension in your Documents folder to your Backup folder.

Creating Directories

The **mkdir** command lets you create directories. To create a directory named NewDirectory in the current working directory:

> **mkdir NewDirectory**

You can also create directories by absolute path. To create a directory named NewDirectory in your Documents folder:

> **mkdir ~/Documents/NewDirectory**

Deleting Files And Folders

Sooner or later, you'll need to delete some files or folders, and the **rm** command will let you get rid of them. To get rid of a file named Book.doc in the current working directory:

rm Book.doc

You can also use **rm** to delete files by their absolute path:

rm /home/jon/Documents/Book.doc

Wildcards also work with **rm**. You can use **rm** to, say, delete every single .doc file on your Documents folder:

rm /home/jon/Documents/*.doc

Needless to say, you will want to be extremely careful when using wildcards with **rm**! If you make an error, you can unintentionally wipe out a large chunk of your files.

You can also remove directories from the command line. To remove an empty directory, use the **rmdir** command:

rmdir NewDirectory

However, note that **rmdir** will only work if the target directory is empty. If it's not, you'll have to clean out any files in the directory before you can delete it with **rmdir**.

Alternatively, you can use the **rm** command with the recursive -r option to delete a directory, all its files, and any subdirectories (along with their files):

rm -r NewDirectory

You'll want to be especially careful when using the rm command with the -r option! You can easily wipe out entire branches of the filesystem, and can lose important data if you're not careful.

Compressing And Uncompressing Files

Modern hard drives are enormous - as of this writing it's common for laptops to have hard drives of three hundred and twenty giga-bytes or more, while desktop machines can have hard drives upwards of a terabyte. So compressing files might not seem like such a big deal. However, compressing files is still useful for creating backups, and many files that you download off the Internet will come in compressed form. When working in the command line environment, you'll need to know how to uncompress these files.

Ubuntu uses the **tar** command to create file "archives", which are a large number of small files combined into one large file for easy storage and copying. The **tar** command dates back to the earliest days of UNIX, and is very efficient. For example, let's say you wanted to create a file named "backup.tar" containing all the files and folders in your Documents folder. You would use the **tar** command with the -c option to create an archive, and the -f option to specify a name for the archive:

tar -cf backup.tar ~/Documents

In short order, **tar** will create the "backup.tar" file. Remember when using the **tar** command to always add the *.tar extension to any filenames, since **tar** will not do so automatically.

However, this new archive isn't compressed at all. It takes up the same amount of space as your ~/Documents folder. To compress it, you'll need to use **tar** with the -z switch, which compresses the archive with gzip compression:

tar -czf backup.tar.gz ~/Documents

You might also want to add the -v option to the command, as well:

tar -czvf backup.tar.gz ~/Documents

The -v command tells **tar** to produce verbose output, which means it tells you exactly what it is doing, and informs you if someting goes wrong.

To unpack files from a **tar** archive, you likewise use the **tar** command, but with the -x switch to *eXtract* the files, rather than the -c switch to *Compress* them:

tar -xvf backup.tar

If a **tar** archive has been compressed with gzip style compression, make sure to add the -z command option to the mix:

tar -xzvf backup.tar.gz

The **tar** command is useful, but complicated. It's somewhat easier to use the **zip** and **unzip** commands. To compress your Documents folder with **zip** into an compressed archive named "backup.zip", use the **zip** command with these options:

zip -r backup.zip ~/Documents

Uncompressing the archive merely takes the **unzip** command:

unzip backup.zip

Note that the files are uncompressed in the same directory as the backup.zip file.

Viewing Files

Moving files, compressing files, and deleting files is useful, but sometimes you'll need to view them as well. A great many files in Ubuntu Linux, especially configuration files, are simply text files, and you can view them with the **cat** command. To view a file named document.txt in the working directory:

cat document.txt

Very often a text document will be too long to fit on a single screen, and will scroll up before you can view the entire thing. You can pipe the output of the **cat** command to the **more** command, which will let you view the file one screen at a time:

cat document.txt | more

"Pipes" in Linux allow you to direct the output of one command to another command, which then acts upon that output.

The **less** command essentially combines the **cat** and the **more** commands, letting you scroll through the text file:

less document.txt

Sometimes you'll just want to view the first few lines of a file. You can do so with the **head** command:

head document.txt

This will display the first five lines of the file. Alternately, you can use the **tail** command to view the final five lines of a file:

tail document.txt

Sometimes you'll want to sort through a document for a particular term, which can take some time. The **grep** command, which searches output, can find a particular search string within the output.

Pipe the output from the **cat** command to **grep**, and it will find any instances of that term:

cat document.txt | grep term

Using Root Powers

As you do things on Ubuntu, you'll quickly notice that a great many areas of the system are restricted. You cannot, for instance, go to the /bin directory and start deleting files at random. This is a good thing - it prevents you from accidentally doing damage to your system (or malicious users from doing damage on purpose).

However, there are times when you'll need to install a program, or edit a configuration file, or perform some other administrative task. To do that, you'll need root-level permissions. The "root" account, also called the superuser account, is the most powerful user on a Linux system. The root account can delete any file and change any setting. For security reasons, the root account is disabled by default on Ubuntu systems, since it presents a tempting target to attackers.

To get around this, Ubuntu uses the **sudo** command, which allows a user to temporarily act as root. To use a command with **sudo**, simply preface it with the **sudo** command:

sudo rm document.txt

The command will ask for your password, and after you enter it, **rm** will run with root-level access.

(Note that only administrative users on a Ubuntu system can use root. By default, the account you create during installation is an administrative user.)

Basic Calculator

Ubuntu also comes with a handy little utility called the **bc** command – the "bc" stands for "basic calculator". The **bc** command lets you perform quick, simple mathematical operations from the command line, which can be easier than reaching for your desktop calculator or firing up a graphical calculator (and if you're using the server version of Ubuntu, no GUI calculator is available, obviously).

To use **bc**, first type this command:

bc

This will take you to the **bc** prompt, and you can now perform mathematical operations. To add two numbers, for instance, type this, and then hit the Enter key:

2 +2

To subtract two numbers, use this syntax:

2 -2

To divide two numbers, use the / key:

2 /2

For multiplication, use the * key:

2 * 2

Use fractions instead of decimals:

2.5 + 1

Once you are finished with bc, type quit to return to the normal command prompt:

quit

Bash Shell Tips

For its command-line interface, Ubuntu uses a program called the bash shell. The term "shell" refers to a program that provides an interface between the user and the operating system. The bash shell is a descendant of the old Bourne sh shell - the name "bash" itself is a pun meaning "Bourne-again shell." There are a number of other shells available, but most people agree that bash is the best one available (opinions can, of course, differ). And bash has a number of useful features.

The first is what's called "command/filename completion." What that means if that you type a partial command or filename, and hit the TAB key, bash will take a good guess at completing the filename or command. Say you have a file named ReallyReallyReallyLongLongLongFileName.txt, and you want to delete it. But you don't want to type out that entire filename. Instead you can just start to type it:

rm ReallyR

And then hit the tab key. The bash shell will finish out the file name for you:

rm R ReallyReallyReallyLongLongLongFileName.txt

The bash shell also has a neat feature called command history. If you hit the Up arrow key on your keyboard, you can scroll back through the history of commands you have used. If you can't remember a long command you just used, or you don't want to retype, this can come in handy.

The bash shell stores your command history in a file named .bash_history in your home folder. To view it, use this command:

cat ~/.bash_history

Note that this file only gets updated when you log out of the system.

Getting Help

There's no getting around it - Linux commands are complicated, and come with a vast array of options and options, and all of that is difficult to remember. Thankfully, Ubuntu Linux comes with a built-in help system - the **man** command. Short for "manual", **man** lets you view the basic usage and options for the command. To use it, simply type **man** and the name of the command whose manual page you want to read:

man ls

This will bring up the manual page for the ls command. You can use the page up and page down keys to navigate through the man page, and once you're finished, pressing the "q" key will return you to the command prompt.

2

FILE AND FOLDER PERMISSIONS AND OWNERSHIP

Newcomers to both Linux in general and Ubuntu in particular are often confused by the way that file permissions and ownership work. Fortunately, these are simple concepts, though they can become complex as different combinations of permissions interact.

Basically, every file and folder on a Ubuntu system can be accessed by three different groups of users - the owning user, the owning group, and everybody else with an account on the system. In Linux file permissions, "ownership" means that the owner, whether the owning user or the owning group, has full control over the file or folder. The owning user and group, obviously, are the particular user and group that have been assigned ownership of that file or folder. (The owner and the root user are the only ones who can change or assign permissions to a file.) Everyone else simply means every other user with an account on the system.

There are three permissions that can be assigned to the owner, the owning group, and everyone else - read, write, and execute.

The Read permission allows you to access the file, but not to delete it or alter it. For example, you could open a document with the

Read permission, but you could not edit it, and you could not delete it.

The Write permission allows you alter or delete a file. To return to our example document, if you have the Write permission, you could delete it or make changes to it. (Ironically, to actually view the document, you also need the Write permission.)

The Execute permission allows you to run a file as a program. Any application or program files need this permission, otherwise they won't work.

When dealing with folders, you need to set both the read and execute permissions to make the folder readable.

How to find permissions on a file? The quickest way is to use the **ls -l** command for the long file listing. As you recall from Chapter 1, the **ls -l** command produces an output that looks something like this:

-rwxrwxrwx 6 bobsmith users 4096 Dec 9 14:56 test.txt

The "-" character at the start of the listing indicates that it's a file; if there's a "d" there instead, then it's a directory. The permissions are listed on the left side of the output - r stands for Read, w stands for Write, and x stands for Execute. It might seem strange that the permissions are repeated three times, but it's not - the first "rwx" group means that the file's owner has the Read, Write, and Execute permissions. The second "rwx" means that the owning group has the Read, Write, and Execute permissions, while the third means that everyone else also gets the Read, Write, and Execute permissions. To put it succinctly, everyone on the Ubuntu system can Read, Write, and Execute that file. From the output, we can also tell that "bobsmith" is the owner of the file, and the group "users" is the owning group.

Let's look at a different example:

-rwxrw-r-- 6 bobsmith users 4096 Dec 9 14:56 test.txt

In this example, we see that the owner of test.txt, user bobsmith, gets the Read, Write, and Execute permissions. The owning group users gets Read and Write, while everyone else only gets the Read permission.

What if the permissions conflict? Like, what if bobsmith has only

Read permission to a file, but everyone else gets Read, Write, and Execute? In that case, bobsmith gets the entire set of Read, Write, and Execute permissions to the file. Permissions are "additive" - that means your permissions to a file are "added up" from the owner's permissions, the group permissions, and everyone else's permissions. Even if you're not the owner of a file, or a member of the owning group, you can still view and alter a file if the everyone group has the Read and Write permissions.

So, how to change a file's permissions? This is done using the **chmod** command. (In Linux, a file's total permissions are called the "mode", so chmod stands for "change mode.") If you want to add the execute permission to the owning user of a file, you would use **chmod** like this (note that in **chmod**, u stands for the owning user):

chmod u+x test.txt

If you wanted to add the execute permission to the owning group:

chmod g+x test.txt

Finally, if you wanted to add the execute permission for everyone on the system:

chmod o+x test.txt

(In **chmod,** o stands for Others, or everyone else on the system.)

And to do all three at once:

chmod u+x,g+x,o+x test.txt

Alternately, to remove permissions, replace the + sign with the - symbol:

chmod u-x,g-x,o-x test.txt

All this typing is rather cumbersome, isn't it? Fortunately, file permissions in Ubuntu Linux have numeric codes - mathematical shorthand, if you will. The Read permission is assigned the number 4, Write the number 2, and Execute the number 1. Having no permissions is represented by a zero. You then calculate the permissions by adding up the numbers. Take this example:

-rwxrw-r-- 6 bobsmith users 4096 Dec 9 14:56 test.txt

The file's owner receives the Read, Write, and Execute permissions, the owning group gets Read and Write, and everyone else gets Read. Since Read is 4, Write is 2, and Execute is 1, the file owner gets a permission of 7. The owning group gets a total of 6, and everyone else gets 4. The permissions can then be expressed numerically as this:

764

And so to set the permissions as 764, you would use the **chmod** command:

chmod 764 test.txt

Much easier to simply type 764, isn't it?

Or to give the owning user full permissions, while denying permissions to both the owning group and everyone else, use this command:

chmod 700 test.txt

Needless to say, this makes using the **chmod** command far less cumbersome. As another example, let us say you wanted to change the permissions of test.txt so that the owner can read, write and execute, the owning group can read and execute, and everyone on the system who is neither the owner nor the owning user can read the file but not write or execute. You would use this chmod command:

chmod 754 test.txt

Assigning permissions is useful, but it's only the first half of managing security for your files and folders. You may also need to sometimes take ownership of files, or to assign them to different owners. Or you may need to assign a file to a different group.

To change the ownership of files, you use the **chown** command. To assign the ownership of the test.txt file to a user named tim:

sudo chown tim test.txt

(You won't need root permissions to change the ownership of files you already own, but you will need it while changing the ownership of files that you don't own.)

To change the group ownership of file, use the **chgrp** command. To assign the group ownership of the test.txt file to a group named marketing:

sudo chgrp marketing test.txt

(You'll almost always need to use **sudo** to change group ownership.)

You might have noticed that all these commands so far only affect one file or directory at one time. How do you change the permissions or ownership of a large number of files at once? Like the **cp** or the **mv** commands, all the commands for managing permissions and ownership work with both the recursive -r option and with wildcards. For instance, to assign ownership of the /test directory, and all its files and subdirectories, to a user named tim:

sudo chown -r tim /test

Using these commands, you can quickly manage both ownership and file permissions on your Ubuntu system.

3

CREATING USERS AND GROUPS

D uring the installation of Ubuntu (whether the Server or the Desktop edition), the installer prompts you to create an administrative account. If you're the only one to use your Ubuntu machine, that should be enough. But if you have more than one person using your Ubuntu system, you'll quickly need additional user accounts to keep everyone's files organized. Assigning permissions is well and good, but you need more than one user account to make permissions work properly. You may also find it necessary to organize those accounts into groups.

In this chapter we'll discuss how to create and delete users, and how to create and delete groups.

Adding Users

To start, let's discuss adding users to your Ubuntu system. You can do this through the GUI, quite easily. Merely go to the Dash, search for "users", and click on the User Accounts icon. This will bring up the Users Settings utility.

From here, you can add and delete user accounts.

However, we've been focusing on how to do things from the

command line, and you can add and remove users and groups quite easily with a few commands. For our example, let's say you want to add a user account for a woman named Caina Amalas to your Ubuntu system.

(Shameless authorial plug: Caina Amalas is the name of the character I've written for a series of sword & sorcery novels - "Child of the Ghosts", "Ghost in the Flames", "Ghost in the Blood", and "Ghost in the Storm.")

To begin, it's best to choose some kind of naming convention for your user accounts. A naming convention sounds fancy, but it just means that you just stick to a consistent way of naming the accounts. Usually, something like the first initial and the last name is best - like "camalas" for Caina Amalas.

To actually create the new camalas user account, use the **useradd** command. You'll need root-level permission to create an account, so you'll have to use useradd with the sudo command:

sudo useradd camalas

However, this command by itself, without any options, is not very useful. It creates the camalas user account, but doesn't assign a display name for the account, nor does it create a home user for camalas. It also doesn't set any variables - for instance, if Caina logs in using the camalas account, she'll get the older sh shell for her command line, instead of the bash shell.

We'll need to add some options to the useradd command to make it more effective. To start, here's how to create a home directory with the command:

sudo useradd -m camalas

The -m option causes **useradd** to create a home directory. Next, we'll add another option, and tell useradd to set bash as camalas's default shell:

sudo useradd -m -s "/bin/bash" camalas

The addition of the -s switch and "/bin/bash" tells **useradd** to set the bash shell for camalas's default shell. Now we'll want to make sure that camalas's display name is properly set as Caina Amalas with the -c option:

sudo useradd -c "Caina Amalas" -m -s "/bin/bash" camalas

With these options, **useradd** creates a new account named camalas, sets the account's display name as Caina Amalas, creates a home directory for the new account, and sets bash for camalas's default shell. (Note that **useradd** has many options, and you can view them all in **useradd's** man page.)

There's one final thing you need to do to allow Caina to log in using the camalas account - you need to set a password for the new account. You can do that using the **passwd** command:

sudo passwd camalas

You can then set a password for camalas. Note that you can also use the **passwd** command, without sudo, to reset the password for your own account.

Ubuntu's user accounts are stored in the /etc/passwd file. It's a plain text file, so you can view it like any other text file:

cat /etc/passwd

You will see a lot of accounts in there, but most of them are for various system services and you needn't concern yourself with them. For actual user accounts, in /etc/passwd you can view the account name, the user id (UID) number, the group id (GUID) of the account's default group, the display name, the location of the home directory, and the default shell.

You might be tempted to manually add user accounts by editing the /etc/passwd file. Do *not* do this! The passwords for user accounts are stored in a restricted file called /etc/shadow, and it needs to stay in sync with /etc/passwd. Manually editing /etc/passwd can mess up your system.

Removing User Accounts

From time to time, you'll want to remove accounts from your Ubuntu system. It's quick and easy to remove an account from the command line. In fact, it's rather less cumbersome than doing it through the GUI.

Before you delete a user account, you might first consider locking it with the **usermod** command. Locking an account disables its password, which means the account can no longer log into the system. For example, to lock the camalas account:

sudo usermod -L camalas

(Note that options, like commands and filenames, are case sensitive, and the -L option must be capitalized.)

If you want to get rid of an account entirely, use the **userdel** command with sudo:

sudo userdel camalas

This command will delete the camalas user account from your system. However, it will not delete camalas's home directory, which means that all her personal files and configuration settings will remain on your system in the /home/camalas folder. To delete both the camalas account and camalas's home folder, use **userdel** with the -r option:

sudo userdel -r camalas

This will delete both the camalas account and camalas's home folder.

Adding Groups

Like user accounts, you can create groups for your users from the Ubuntu command line. There are a couple of different ways to create groups in Ubuntu, and both ways are valid. First, you can use the **groupadd** command to add a group named ghosts:

sudo groupadd ghosts

Alternatively, you could use the **addgroup** command:

sudo addgroup ghosts

Both commands do the same thing, but have different potential options, if you wish to peruse their man pages.

(Second shameless authorial plug: in the "Sword & Sorceress" stories and "Ghosts" novels, Caina belongs to the Ghosts, the spies of the Emperor of Nighmar.)

Like user accounts, Ubuntu stores all its groups in a plain text file, /etc/group. To view this file:

cat /etc/group

Most of the groups in there are system groups and can be safely ignored. It will seem like all of your user accounts are simultaneously listed in the group file as well - these are actually the primary groups of your user accounts (Ubuntu creates a group for each of your user accounts, and assigns the user account that group as its primary group). Any groups that you create will appear on the bottom of the file.

Adding Users To Groups

Once you've created your group, you can add users to it. Again, there are a couple of different ways to do so. The first way is with the **useradd** command. To add the camalas account to the ghosts group:

sudo useradd camalas ghosts

You can also use the **usermod** command to add a user to a group:

sudo usermod -G ghosts -a camalas

Removing Users From Groups

To remove an account from a group, use the **userdel** command:

sudo userdel camalas ghosts

This will remove camalas from the ghosts group.

Deleting Groups

To remove a group, use the **groupdel** command:

sudo groupdel ghosts

This will eliminate the ghosts group, even if it still has members.

Note that you cannot remove the primary group of any user without first either removing that user account from the group, or deleting the user account. (Remember that Ubuntu creates a group named after each of your user accounts.)

4

INSTALLING SOFTWARE

F or people used to the Microsoft Windows system, it can be to
difficult to figure out how to install software on a Ubuntu
system. Usually, on a Windows machine, you download the
installer file from the website, double-click on it, and follow the steps
suggested by the install wizard. Or you insert the CD or DVD into
your optical drive and follow the AutoPlay prompt, or navigate to the
DVD's root menu through Windows Explorer and double-click on
the SETUP.EXE file. One of the strengths of the Microsoft Windows
is the relative ease of installing software on a Windows computer, and
the enormous library of software available for Windows. (In fact, the
ease of installing software on Windows can be a weakness - consider
how easy it is to catch malware on a Windows box.) Unfortunately,
this vast library of software (usually) will not work on Ubuntu.
(Unless you have Wine, which we'll discuss in Chapter 18.)

Fortunately, Ubuntu is a Linux distribution. While it may not
have access to the Windows software ecosystem, it nonetheless has
access to the vast library of Linux applications and utilities. And as an
added bonus, many of these applications are free - both free to use
and free to alter and distribute without legal encumbrance.

There are six basic ways to install software programs on your

Ubuntu system: the Ubuntu Software application, Synaptic Package Manager, .deb installer files, the command line, Snaps, and Flatpak. All of them are fairly easy to use. Server-level applications usually take some more work, but installing end-user applications is straightforward. Our focus in this book is on the command line, but we'll also go through the graphical ways of installing applications.

Note that you'll need an admin account on your Ubuntu system to install software - the default account you create during installation counts as an admin account.

Repositories

However, before we start, you'll need to understand the concept of a software repository. Basically, a software repository is a server on the Internet where the installer packages for software programs are stored. ("Packages" are software installers that are pre-compiled to work with a particular operating system, usually specific versions of Linux.) Client computers can then access those repositories, download the packages, and install the programs. This more efficient than, say, distributing software via CD or DVD, or by downloading the installer from a web server.

Canonical operates a number of software repositories, divided into roughly four groups. The "main" repository holds open source software maintained by Canonical. The "universe" repository contains open source software from other groups. The "restricted" repository holds non-free software necessary for device drivers (there is a lack of free Linux drivers for video cards and wireless network adapters, in particular). Finally, the "multiverse" repository contains non-free software restricted by either copyright or legal issues, or both.

It's possible to add additional repositories to your system - we'll discuss how to do that shortly.

The Ubuntu Software Application

Canonical first introduced the Ubuntu Software Center in October of 2009 with Ubuntu 9.10. Since then it's undergone considerable improvements, and been rebranded as the Ubuntu Software application. To launch Ubuntu Software, go to the Dash, search for "Ubuntu Software" and click on the icon for Ubuntu Software. It's also pinned to the Launcher in the default configuration of Ubuntu. (Obviously, Ubuntu Software is only available in the Desktop edition of Ubuntu, not Server.)

By clicking on Ubuntu Software's "Installed" button, you can see the software already installed on your system, along with the history of installs and uninstalls. In "All Software" button, you see software sorted into simple categories - Office, Graphics, Sound & Video, and so forth. It also includes a Featured Applications category, where some of the best applications for Ubuntu are featured. Click on any one of these categories, and you'll see the individual applications listed within. If you click on the More Info button, you'll see more information about the application. This varies by application, and how much information the developers bothered to post. Usually, you'll see an extended description, some screenshots, and a link to the application's web site.

You can also search for applications, both through the entire catalog and within specific categories, by using the search box in the upper right-hand corner of the window. You can search for applications either by specific name, or by terms in their descriptions.

Installing applications is a breeze; merely select the application you want, and click Install. After you enter your password to authenticate, Ubuntu Software will link up with the Ubuntu repositories, and download and install the application you want.

Ubuntu Software is far and away the easiest way to install software on Ubuntu - but it doesn't work from the command line.

Synaptic Package Manager

The second way to install software through the GUI is using the Synaptic Package Manager. As of Ubuntu 11.10 Oneiric Ocelot, Synaptic is no longer included with the default Ubuntu installation. You can quickly install Synaptic either through the Software application or from the command line with this command:

sudo apt-get install synaptic

Synaptic is essentially a graphical interface to apt, the Advanced Packaging Tool, which is a utility that handles the installation of software on Debian Linux and Debian-derived distributions (such as Ubuntu). You can launch Synaptic (after installing Synaptic) by clicking on the Activities Overview and searching for Synaptic in the search field. Synaptic needs root powers to run, so you'll need to enter your password to confirm. After you do, Synaptic will open.

Synaptic's graphical interface isn't quite as friendly as Ubuntu Software Center's, and can be confusing to use. Synaptic's big advantage is that it lists every single package available in any software repositories you have configured your system to use. Even better, the list is searchable - if you don't know the name of a package, you can search for it by name or description. For example, if you wanted to install Virtualbox, but didn't know the name of the package, you could search for any packages with "Virtualbox" in their name, and find what you need in short order.

Synaptic will also let you upgrade all the installed programs on your system at once, assuming that upgrades are in fact available in the software repositories. The "Mark All Upgrades" button will search out any upgrades, and mark the packages that can be upgraded. You can then hit the Apply button to download and install the upgrade packages.

(Note that you cannot use Synaptic and the Ubuntu Software application at the same time, since they will both try to lock the installation directory. You may have both installed on your system, but cannot use both simultaneously.)

Deb Packages

The Ubuntu software repositories store a vast selection of software, but they do not contain every last available application for Ubuntu. Sometimes developers prefer not to keep their software in the repositories for a variety of reasons, or prefer to make the application available themselves. Very often the installer for such a program will be distributed in what's called a deb file. The developer will make the deb file available for download on their website. (As of this writing, Google keeps most of its Ubuntu-compatible applications - Chrome and the like - available as deb files on the download section of the Google site.)

To install an application from a deb file, simply download it and double-click it to run. (Ironically, despite the differences we discussed earlier, this is almost like installing software for Windows.) Depending on how the deb file is put together, you'll either be redirected to the Ubuntu Software application, or presented with a the graphical front end for the dpkg tool (the application that installs deb packages - we'll discuss it more in the next section). In either case, you'll hit the Install button, enter your password to confirm, and the application will install itself on your system.

Installing Software From The Command Line

Synaptic itself is only a graphical interface for the Advanced Packaging Tool, or "apt", as it is more commonly known. The apt tool, as we mentioned above, automates the installation of software on Debian and Debian-derived systems (like Ubuntu) by downloading the package files from the repository and installing them. You can use apt to install, upgrade, and remove software from the command line, and apt makes the process quick, easy, and painless.

(Note that you CANNOT use apt while Synaptic is also open, since both Synaptic and apt need to lock the /var/lib/dpkg/lock directory while installing software. This is a common mistake - people will look up a package's name in Synaptic, and then go to the Terminal to install it, forgetting to close Synaptic first.)

To use apt, you need admin rights to your system, as well as the name of the package you want to install. Let's say that you want to install the VLC media player application on your computer. The name of VLC's installer package is simply "vlc", and it's in the Ubuntu repositories. To install it, you'd simply use this command:

sudo apt-get install vlc

(Installing software almost always must be done as root.)

Enter your password to authenticate, and apt-get will download VLC from the repositories and install it for you. If you change your mind, apt also makes it easy to remove software:

sudo apt-get remove vlc

(Again, you need root permissions to remove software, along with the name of the application.)

Like Synaptic, apt can also upgrade any packages on your system that have upgrades available in the repositories. First, use apt-get to update your system's listing of its repositories:

sudo apt-get update

This usually takes a few minutes to run. After the command finishes, you can then upgrade any packages with upgrades available:

sudo apt-get upgrade

This command might take a while, depending on how many upgrades are available (and how large the upgrades are). But after it's done, the software on your system will be up to date.

Finally, you can also install deb packages from the command line, which is a necessity if you want to install a deb package in the Server edition of Ubuntu. To install a deb file called installer.deb:

sudo dpkg -i installer.deb

Likewise, **dpkg** can also remove software with the -r option:

sudo dpkg -r installer.deb

Install Software From A Personal Package Archive

Some developers take a halfway point between putting their application in the Ubuntu repositories or distributing as a deb file. They instead create a "personal package archive", commonly abbreviated as a PPA, to house their application's installer. Users can then connect to the PPA and use apt to download and install the application. Very often this happens with new applications that haven't yet been included in the Ubuntu repositories, or applications that are still in beta or even the alpha testing stages.

(Before going any further, we should emphasize that you should install software from a PPA only if the developer is reputable - an unscrupulous software developer could create a fake PPA with installers for malicious software.)

For example, say you want to install an application called "viewer". It's not available in the Ubuntu repositories, but the developer maintains a PPA called "viewer/viewer-releases". Here's how you would add the PPA to your Ubuntu system:

sudo add-apt-repository ppa:viewer/viewer-releases

Then update your system's listing of the repositories, to force it to index the new PPA:

sudo apt-get update

After that command is finished, you are now free to download and install the viewer application:

sudo apt-get install viewer

Snaps

Snappy is a new method of installing software on a Ubuntu computer. It is a "universal" package management system, designed to work on all Linux distributions. (Specifically, any Linux distributions that include the snapd daemon.) The idea is that "Snaps", applications designed for Snappy, can run on any system that supports Snappy, meaning that applications are easier to install, upgrade, and run. It was originally developed for the aborted Ubuntu

Phone and Unity projects, but has since made its way into the desktop distribution.

Snappy was included in Ubuntu as of Ubuntu 16.04 Xenial Xerus, and has been included in every version of Ubuntu desktop since then. Snaps are installed and managed using the Terminal **snap** command.

First, to list all Snaps presently installed on your Ubuntu system, use this command:

sudo snap list

To locate a specific Snap in the Snappy app store, use the **snap find** command. For example:

sudo snap find inkscape

This will show any information about the Snap application in question.

To install a Snap, use this command:

sudo snap install inkscape

This command will download and install the popular Inkscape vector graphic editor. Depending on the size of the application in question, the download and installation may take some time. Once Inkscape is installed, you can find and launch it from the Dash.

To update a Snap, use the **refresh snap** command. For instance, this command will update Inkscape:

sudo snap refresh inkscape

This command will update all installed Snaps on your Ubuntu computer:

sudo snap refresh all

Finally, if you wish to uninstall a Snap application from your computer, use the snap remove command. This example will remove the Inkscape application:

SUDO **snap remove inkscape**

Flatpak

Like Snaps, Flatpak is a universal application system, designed to work on every Linux system that can support the underlying Flatpak software. Flatpak applications are sandboxed, meaning they cannot alter or interfere with the operating system or control system hardware without explicit user consent. As of Ubuntu 18.04 Bionic Beaver, Flatpak support is included in Ubuntu, though it has to be enabled first.

To enable Flatpak, go to a Terminal window and run this command:

sudo apt install gnome-software-plugin-flatpak

After this command finishes running, execute this command to add the Flatpak repository:

flatpak   remote-add   –if-not-exists   flathub https://flathub.org/repo/flathub.flatpakrepo

After this command finishes, restart your system.

Once your system comes back up, you can install Flatpak apps. You can do through so a web browser if you visit the Flathub website at https://flathub.org. Simply navigate to the application you want to use and click the Install button. The installer file will download and open in the Ubuntu Software application, and you can install it from there.

Alternatively, you can install Flatpak applications from the command line if you know the package name. For example, to install GIMP from the command line, you would use this command:

flatpak   install   https://flathub.org/repo/appstream/org.gimp.GIMP.flatpakref

This will download and install the GIMP on your Ubuntu system as a Flatpak application.

5

CHECKING MEMORY AND DISK SPACE USAGE

When it comes to dealing with computers (whether Ubuntu, Windows, or Mac OS X systems), there is one infallible rule - there's never enough memory or disk space. Granted, the situation has gotten better than the old days of DOS, when you had only 640 kilobytes of memory to use. Personal computers have gotten more powerful, and as of this writing you can buy a laptop computer with four gigabytes of memory and a five hundred gigabyte hard drive for about $300 to $400 USD (even less if the computer is a desktop). So for the average user, carefully managing your personal computer's memory and disk space isn't quite as critical as it once was.

However, you'll still want to keep an eye on memory and disk usage. If your Ubuntu system slows down, you'll want to know why, and examining resource usage can give you a clue as to the cause. If your hard drive fills up, you'll want to find which files are taking the most room. And if you are managing a Ubuntu Server system with multiple users accessing it simultaneously, you will definitely want to keep a close eye on resource usage, lest one user bring the server to a crashing halt.

In this chapter we'll look at how to monitor Ubuntu's usage of system resources, both with graphical and command line tools.

System Monitor

System Monitor is a utility that provides a wealth of real-time information about the status of your system. From System Monitor, you can see how much RAM and hard drive space your system has free. You can also view graphs charting CPU usage, the amount of memory used by the various processes running on your system, and the amount of free space on any additional disks (like flash drives or external hard drives) attached to your computer.

To launch System Monitor, click on the Dash and search for it in the search field. Click on the program's icon, and System Manager should launch in short order.

System Monitor has four tabs, each presenting different information, that we'll look at from left to right.

"System" is the first tab, and as the name suggests, it presents basic information about your system. At the top you'll see your system's hostname, followed your system's version of Ubuntu and version of the Linux kernel. You'll also see the total amount of RAM your system has installed, along with the type and speed of your CPU. Below that, you'll see the available disk space on your hard drive (if you have multiple hard drives installed, it will show the free space on the drive that has your Ubuntu installation).

"Processes" is the next tab. A "process" is the technical term for any program running on your system, whether a background daemon (a program that provides services), or any programs that you or any other users launch. The Processes tab has a number of columns that provide useful information. The first column, "Process Name", provides the name of the process. The "% CPU" tab shows the amount of the CPU's processing time the process is consuming. The "ID" column shows the process's ID number, which comes in handy if you need to force it to end from the command line (which we will describe in Chapter 22). The "Memory" column shows the amount of memory the process is using. Finally, the Processes tab has an End Process button in the lower-right hand corner, which you can use to forcibly shut down unresponsive processes.

The third tab, "Resources", provides three real-time graphs. The first graph, "CPU History", shows the amount of CPU time being consumed. If you have a multi-core processor (as most computers do nowadays), the graph will represent the different CPU cores with different colors. The second graph, "Memory and Swap History", shows the amount of RAM and swap file space being used. ("Swap file" refers to virtual memory, a partition on your hard drive that Ubuntu uses as temporary RAM if the real RAM fills up.) The final graph, "Network History", shows the amount of incoming and outgoing traffic to your system's network adapter.

The final tab "File Systems" shows any file systems – that is, disks – attached to your Ubuntu system. This includes hard drives, optical disks (like CDs and DVDs), USB external hard drives, and USB flash drivers. The columns show the actual device names for the drives (usually something like /dev/sda1), the mount point (where the device is mounted in the filesystem), the type of filesystem, and the amount of space on the device, both total space and free space.

System Monitor offers a lot of useful information in one convenient place, but it's a graphical application, which means that it doesn't work from the command line. To check this information from the command line, you'll need to use the top command, which we'll discuss in the next section.

The Top Command

The top command has been around forever, and is included in practically every variant of Linux. Ubuntu is no exception. The top command displays a variety of useful statistics, including the "top" users of CPU time (hence the command's name). To launch top, simply type the command at the command prompt:

top

Once launched, top stays running, displaying statistics in real time. Processes are listed by their process ID number, along the name of the command that started the process. There's a lot of information listed in top, so let's take a look at the available statistics:

PID: A process's process ID number.

USER: The process's owner. Processes owned by root are usually system processes, and should be left alone unless they cause problems.

PR: The process's priority, which determines how much attention the CPU will give this process over other processes. The lower the number, the higher the priority.

NI: The nice value of the process, which affects its priority.

VIRT: How much virtual memory the process is using.

RES: How much physical RAM the process is using, measured in kilobytes.

SHR: How much shared memory the process is using.

S: The current status of the process (zombied, sleeping, running, uninterruptedly sleeping, or traced).

%CPU: The percentage of the processor time used by the process.

%MEM: The percentage of physical RAM used by the process.

TIME+: How much processor time the process has used.

COMMAND: The name of the command that started the process.

Of course, you may want to sort the top display by a certain category from least to greatest. This is especially useful when you want to figure out what process is hogging the most CPU time or memory. Hitting the 't' key will sort the processes by CPU time. Hitting 'l' will sort by load average, and 'm' by memory info.

Like System Monitor, you can also use top to kill uncooperative processes. To do this, you'll need to make note of the process ID you want to kill. Hit the "k" key while top is running, and the utility will ask you to input a process ID number. Input the number, hit Enter, and then hit Enter again when it asks if you want to kill the process (top assumes you mean "yes" when you hit enter). The top utility will then kill the process.

Once you've finished with top, hit the q key to exit and return to the command line.

Check Disk Space Usage

The top command can do quite a lot, but there's one thing that System Monitor can do that top can't – it can show the amount of used disk space. And keeping track of the used space on your hard drive is important. Granted, these days computers come with enormous hard drives - a capacity of one or even two terabytes in a desktop machine is quite common. Of course, the size of popular files has only gotten larger (video takes up an enormous amount of space), making it all the easier to fill up your hard drive. And filling up your hard drive can cause all sorts of unintended problems, especially on a server system.

Fortunately, there are several commands you can use to track disk space usage from the command line in Ubuntu.

The first command is **df**, which produces an output like this:

/dev/sda1   31621016   3364900   26649820   12% /

You'll notice like the Filesystems tab in System Monitor, the df command lists all the filesystems on your computer. The first number is the total size of the drive. The second is the used space. The third is the available space, and the final number is the percentage of space used. However, the numbers are in 1 kilobyte blocks, which makes the difficult to read without mental mathematics. To make the output more readable, use **df** with the -h option:

/dev/sda1   31G   3.3G   26G   12% /

You'll notice that the sizes are now in gigabytes (or megabytes, depending on the size of the filesystem), which is much more readable.

You might also need to check the size of an individual folder, since the ls command, even with the -l option doesn't bother to list the size of folders. (Technically, directories in Linux are also files, so the **ls -l** command only lists the size of the file representing the directory without any of the directory's contents.) To find the size of a folder from the commmand line, use the **du** command with the -s and -h options:

du -sh ~

The command will list the size of the targeted folder in megabytes or gigabytes, as appropriate.

Check Memory Usage

The top command does a pretty good job of seeing which processes are using the most memory. It does not, however, give an overview of your system's entire memory. To do so, you need to use the **free** command, which generates an output like this:

Mem: 1025700   340708   684992   0   38904   156368

The first three numbers are the most important - they list the total amount of RAM, the amount used, and the amount currently free. The RAM is listed in bytes which, unless you're really good at mental math, makes it rather hard to read. Fortunately, you can use the -m option with **free** to display the totals in megabytes instead of bytes, generating an output like this:

Mem: 1001   501   500   0   64   277

The numbers are roughly the same as before, but they're expressed in megabytes now, not bytes, which usually makes for easier reading. You can also use the -k and -g switches to express the values in kilobytes and megabytes, if you prefer.

6

EDITING TEXT FILES WITH VI

We've spent the last few chapters covering the basics of Ubuntu Linux - the command line, file permissions, users and groups, and managing system resources. We're now ready to move on to more advanced topics, such as how to configure Ubuntu for a variety of server roles. Ubuntu can be configured to perform almost any server task, offering a powerful server platform at very low cost.

First, however, we have to talk about configuration files, and how to edit them.

Configuration files on the Microsoft Windows platform are almost always *.ini files, or hex files, or binary files that you cannot alter without special programs. In contrast, configuration files on Linux are usually simple text files that you can alter with any text editor program. Ubuntu comes with a graphical text editor, the gedit program, that lets you edit text while providing a full GUI menu with copy and paste and so forth.

However, gedit doesn't work from the command line, and it *definitely* doesn't work in the Server Edition of Ubuntu, which does not include a GUI. Therefore it is vital to learn a command line editor if you want to configure Ubuntu as a server.

There are a number of command line editors available for Ubuntu - nano, Richard Stallman's Emacs, vi, and others. I think vi is the simplest to use, so this chapter will focus on using the vi editor. Granted, opinions can and do differ on the best editor to use - a flame war on the relative merits of Emacs and vi has been going for decades.

What Is Vi?

The vi editor has been around for a long time. It grew out of a series of UNIX text editors in the 1960s and the 1970s, with the first version developed by programmer Bill Joy in the late 1970s. Later, vi was praised for its small memory footprint, which meant it could be used on systems with low amounts of available memory.

The variant of vi included with Ubuntu is actually vim, which stands for "vi Improved." Vim was developed by a programmer named Bram Moolenaar in the early 1990s. Today, vim is generally the most popular variant of vi, and is included with most Linux distributions.

However, the vi command is still symbolically linked to vim, so typing vi into Ubuntu's command line will launch vim.

Launching Vi

Launching vi is simply a matter of typing the command:

vi

This will take you to an empty file, and you can create text files from here.

However, you'll often use vi to view or edit an existing text file. If you wanted to use vi to open a file named test.txt:

vi test.txt

The vi editor will then launch with the test.txt file open.

You can also use vi to create new files. For instance, if you wanted to use vi to create a text file named newfile.txt:

vi newfile.txt

However, note that the file isn't actually written to disk (and therefore doesn't exist permanently) until you write it to disk. We'll discuss how to do that in the next section.

Vi Modes

Vi is not like a modern word processor, in that you can't simply fire it up, sit down, and start typing. Vi has different modes of operation, each of which has a different function. If you think of vi as a Swiss army knife, then the modes are the different kinds of blades and attachments within the knife.

Vi has four modes:

-Normal mode. Vi starts in default mode, and you can delete text from within normal mode.

-Command mode. This lets you save your text file.

-Insert mode. This lets you type fresh text into your file.

-Replace mode. This is similar to Insert mode, but you can over-type text, which you can't do in Insert mode.

Let's take a closer look at each of the modes.

Normal Mode

Vi starts in Normal mode. Normal mode lets you navigate around the text file by moving the cursor with the up and down arrow keys, along with the Page Up and Page Down keys. Pressing the HOME key takes you to the beginning of the file, and pressing END moves you to the end. You can also use Normal mode to delete text within the file, from single characters all the way up to entire lines. Normal mode also offers a search feature, allowing you to quickly locate specific search terms within the file.

First, let's take a look at the commands to delete text within Normal mode.

-Pressing **dw** deletes the word immediately after the cursor. This command also deletes the space following the word.

-Pressing **de** also deletes the word immediately following the cursor. Unlike **dw**, however, it does not delete the space following the word.

-Pressing **d$** deletes from the cursor to the end of the current line.

-Pressing **dd** deletes the entire current line.

-Pressing **p** inserts the text from the last deletion after the current location of cursor. Essentially, in conjunction with the deletion commands, this lets you cut and paste within vi.

-Pressing **u** undoes the last action. Trust me, if you've made a mistake while editing a text file with vi, this can definitely come in handy.

-Pressing **CTRL-G** (the CTRL and the G keys at the same time) displays a status bar at the bottom of the screen. The status bar will display the name of the file, whether or not it has been modified since the last time it was saved, which line and column the cursor currently occupies, and how far into the file you are as a percentage.

-Pressing **/** (forward slash) activates the search function. Type a search term and hit enter, and vi will take you to the first instance of the search term. You can then hit the N key to jump to the next instance of the term.

Once you've deleted items from your text file, you may want to save the changes. We'll show you how to do that next in Command mode.

Command Mode

Normal mode lets you navigate around a text file and delete parts of it, but Command mode lets you save your file. Command mode also lets you quit vi, with or without saving your text file first.

To access Command mode, you must first be in Normal mode. Press the colon key (the : key), and you'll be moved to Command mode. You'll know you're in Command mode when you see a : prompt at the bottom of your screen.

Let's look at the commands you can use while in Command mode (note that you must hit the Enter key after typing these commands):

-Pressing the **w** key writes the current text file to disk. This basically means that the file is saved. If you used vi to create a new file, it is written to disk. If you're editing a file, any changes you made to the file are written to the disk. So only use the **w** command if you're absolutely sure you want to save your changes.

-Pressing the **q** key quits vi and returns you to the command prompt. Note that the **q** command will only work if you haven't made any changes to the text file, or if you've made changes but haven't yet saved them to disk.

-Pressing the **q!** keys forces vi to quit, even if you haven't yet written your current text file to disk. This generally gets used when you've made serious mistakes editing a text file and want to start over from scratch. Remember, any changes you made to the text file are discarded, so only use **q!** if you don't want to save your changes.

-Pressing **wq**, as you might expect, combines the **w** and **q** commands. This command writes your file to disk, and then exits vi.

-Typing exit and then hitting the Enter key does the same thing as **wq**.

Insert Mode

Insert mode, as the name suggests, lets you insert text into the text file. Access Insert mode by pressing the **INSERT** key while in Normal mode. You can also enter Insert mode by pressing the **I** key or the **S** key while in Normal mode.

Insert mode works much like most people expect a word processor to work – you type, and the text appears on the screen. You can also use the arrow keys and Page Up and Page Down to navigate around the file, even while in Insert mode.

Text is inserted to the right of the cursor. Note that Insert mode doesn't overwrite text when you type. Any text that already exists is pushed to the right as you add new text.

To return to Normal mode from Insert mode, press the **ESC** key.

Note that you can't enter Command mode from within Insert mode, since Insert mode interprets the colon character (:) as simply another text character and adds it to the file.

Replace Mode

The final mode of vi, Replace mode, works almost exactly like Insert mode, but with one key difference. Replace mode overwrites text as you replace it.

To access Replace mode, press the **INSERT** key while you are in Insert mode. This will shift you to Replace mode. As you type, you'll notice that preexisting text it overwritten, rather than moved to the right.

Once you've finished working in Replace mode, you can return to Normal mode by hitting the **ESC** key.

Note that you can't enter Command mode from within Replace mode, since Replace mode interprets the colon character (:) as simply another text character and adds it to the file.

Why Learn Vi?

Compared to graphical editors like gedit, or even graphical word processors like LibreOffice or AbiWord, vi seems hideously complicated. Why learn it?

Because, as we mentioned above, you'll need it when working from the command line in an environment with no GUI. If you want to use Ubuntu as a server, you'll need to learn vi (or another command line editor). Besides, vi is actually pretty easy to learn. After some practice, you'll be editing text files with ease.

7

NETWORK SETTINGS AND ASSIGNING A STATIC IP

T he day of the stand-alone personal computer is long past. These days, practically every personal computer, whether a desktop or laptop, will spend most of its life connected to the Internet. Ubuntu Linux is no different. If you want to browse the Internet and check email from a desktop or laptop with Ubuntu, you'll need to connect it to the Internet. And if you have a server running Ubuntu, you'll need to connect it to either the Internet or a local-area network (LAN). Very often you'll need to give a Ubuntu server system a static IP address, as well, so client systems can consistently find it.

In this chapter we'll discuss how to work with IP addresses in Ubuntu Linux, and how to assign a static IP address to your system.

The Basics Of Ip Addresses

The letters "IP" stand for Internet Protocol, and the Internet Protocol is part of the TCP/IP (Transmission Control Protocol/Internet Protocol) suite, a group of related protocols that lay down the rules for how computers communicate over networks, both over LANs and the larger Internet. An IP address, therefore, is a (theoretically) unique address assigned to a computer. It's a bit like a street address - it lets other computers send traffic to and receive traffic from your system. An IP address consists of four groups of numbers separated by dots:

192.168.1.1

However, the dominant version of the IP protocol is Version 4, commonly referred to as IPv4. Under IPv4, there are only 4.6 billion IP addresses available, and the unclaimed IP addresses ran out in 2011. (IPv6, which has many more available addresses, will eventually replace IPv4, but for now, IPv4 remains dominant.) There are obviously far more computers, phones, routers, switches, and other networked devices in the world than 4.6 billion, so how do all these devices receive IP addresses?

The answer is a "private IP address." Certain blocks of IP addresses have been reserved for use in private networks. These blocks, using a technology called Network Address Translation (NAT), are then "translated" to public IP addresses. This has extended the lifetime of the available IPv4 address space for decades. The ranges of the reserved private addresses are:

10.0.0.0 - 10.255.255.255

172.16.0.0 - 172.31.255.255

192.168.0.0 - 192.168.255.255

Odds are, your computer has an IP address in one of those ranges as part of a private network (even if it's just a private network generated by your wireless router).

IP address also have a "subnet mask". A subnet mask defines which parts of the IP address designate the network, and which part designates the individual computer. Let's say the IP address of 192.168.1.1 from above has a subnet mask like this:

255.255.255.0

That means the 192.168.1 part of the address indicates the network, while the final 1 indicates the computer.

IP addresses usually include a "broadcast" address. Any traffic sent to the broadcast address is directed to every single computer in the local network. A broadcast address has a "255" as its final number, so a computer with a 192.168.1.1 address will have a broadcast address of 192.168.1.255.

Lastly, IP addresses usually (but not always) come with a "default gateway". The default gateway is the address your computer sends traffic destined for anywhere outside the local network segment. Like, say you want to visit Google with your web browser. Your computer recognizes that Google isn't on the 192.168.1.* network, and so forwards the request to the default gateway, which then sends the traffic on to Google. (This is an simplification, but adequate for our purposes.)

Next, let's discuss a basic overview of IPv6 networking.

A Summary Of Ipv6 Networking

As we mentioned earlier, in 2011 the world ran out of available IPv4 address. Since there are only about 4.6 billion IPv4 addresses, and there are far more networked devices in the world than 4.6 billion (think of all those computers, smartphones, tablets, routers, Internet TVs, printers, and other devices), a solution had to be found. Version 6 of the Internet Protocol, IPv6, is that solution. As of this writing, IPv6 is still on the fringes, but in a few years it will supersede IPv4 entirely.

IPv4 used a 32-bit addressing scheme, with four eight-bit groups to identify the computer and the network. IPv6, by contrast, uses a 128-bit binary number for the address. IPv4 maxed out at 4.6 billion available addresses. IPv6 has a theoretical limit of 2^{128} addresses. In simple numerals, that's about 340,282,366,920,938,463,463,374,607,431,768,211,456 addresses.

Given that this means we could theoretically assign an IPv6 address to every single atom on the earth, and then have enough addresses left over to assign addresses to the atoms of another hundred Earth-sized planets, it is unlikely that we shall run out of IPv6 addresses anytime soon.

A typical IPv6 address will look something like this:

. . .

2001:0DB8:85A3:0042:0000:8A2E:0370:7334

HOWEVER, you will rarely see an entire IPv6 spelled out like this. There are a number of shorthand ways to display an IPv6 address. The first to eliminate any leading zeroes in each of address blocks:

2001:DB8:85A3:42:0:8A2E:370:7334

ADDITIONALLY, you can also use a pair of colons (::) to represent a long string of zeroes. So our original address could be further shortened down to this:

2001:DB8:85A3:42::8A23:370:7334

GRANTED, this is still a lot to type (or to read to a support technician over the phone), but still easier that typing out the entire address.

IPv6 addresses do not have subnet masks the way that IPv4 addresses do. Instead an IPv6 address has a "subnet prefix", which identifies how much of the IPv6 address identifies the local network segment and how much identifies the individual computer. Usually, the first 64 bits of the IPv6 address (the first four blocks of four digits) identifies the network segment, and the second 64 bits identifies the individual computer (and this is usually derived from the computer's MAC address).

There are three main kinds of IPv6 addresses assigned to personal computers. The first is a Global IPv6 address, which is equivalent to a public IPv4 address. Global addresses are designed to be accessible from the Internet, and website or public network services will have a Global address. Global addresses always start with either a 2 or a 3.

A Link-local address is the second major kind of address. A Link-local address basically works the same as an APIPA address, in that a computer assigns itself a Link-local address when it hasn't been given a static address or is able to contact a DHCP server. A Link-local address always starts with fe8.

Finally, the third major kind of IPv6 address given to personal computer is a Site-local address. A Site-local address is equivalent to the private IPv4 addresses we described above. Like IPv4 private addresses, Site-local IPv6 addresses are intended to be used in an organization's private networks, and are usually not accessible from the Internet. Site-local IPv6 addresses always start with fec0. Not many organizations are currently using Site-local addresses, but as IPv4 becomes increasingly obsolete, more organizations will switch to them.

Like IPv4, IPv6 also offers a local loopback address. The local loopback address for IPv6 is this:

0000:0000:0000:0000:0000:0000:0000:0001

But remember that a string of zeroes can be shortened with a pair of colons. So the local loopback address for IPv6 is usually displayed like this:

::1

That is much easier to type!

Next, let's see how to find both your IPv4 and IPv6 address on a Ubuntu computer. First, though, we'll need to discuss the difference between the net-tools set of command line utilities and the iproute2 suite.

net-tools VERSUS iproute2

For years, Ubuntu used the traditional net-tools set of command-line utilities for network tasks. However, as IPv6 has begun to replace IPv6, the net-tools utilities haven't been able to keep pace. Consequently, Ubuntu 17.04 Zesty Zapus did not include the increasingly obsolete net-tools utilities but instead the newer iproute2 utilities.

In the next section, we will include both the old net-tools commands and the iproute2 commands.

That said, if you want to install the net-tools set of utilities on Ubuntu 17.04 Zesty Zapus, you can do so at any time with this command:

sudo apt-get install net-tools

Find Your Ip Address

It's actually much easier to find your IP address from the command line in Ubuntu than from the graphical interface. Simply go to a command prompt and type this command:

ifconfig

The ifconfig command will generate an output that looks something like this:

There's quite a bit of information here, but most of it is useful. The "eth0" refers to the first Ethernet connection on your system. The "indet addr" displays your system's IP address, while "Mask" shows the subnet mask. "HWaddr" shows your Ethernet adapter's MAC (Media Access Control) address, which is (theoretically) unique to each adapter. (Some wireless networks require you to supply your MAC address before allowing your system to connect.) The "inet6 addr" displays your system's IPv6 address, if available.

On Ubuntu 17.04 Zesty Zapus, the equivalent command with the iproute2 utilities would be:

ip addr

You can pipe the output from the ifconfig command to grep to quickly find the specific item you want. Let's say you just want to find the IP address:

ifconfig | grep inet

This time, the output will look like this, and you can quickly pick your IP address from the mix:

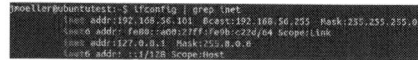

On Ubuntu 17.04 Zesty Zapus, the equivalent command with the iproute2 utilities would be:

ip addr | grep inet

Likewise, you can quickly find your computer's MAC address with ifconfig and grep:

ifconfig | grep HWaddr

You can easily pick out your MAC address from the output:

```
jmoeller@ubuntutest:~$ ifconfig | grep HWaddr
eth0      Link encap:Ethernet  HWaddr 08:00:27:9b:c2:2d
```

On Ubuntu 17.04 Zesty Zapus, the equivalent command with the iproute2 utilities would be:

ip addr | grep ether

How do you find your system's default gateway? You need to use another command for that:

ip route

The ip route command will spit out an output like this:

```
jmoeller@ubuntutest:~$ ip route
169.254.0.0/16 dev eth0  scope link  metric 1000
192.168.56.0/24 dev eth0  proto kernel  scope link  src 192.168.56.101
```

Look for the line that begins "default via." Your system's default gateway will be the IP address after those two words.

On Ubuntu 17.04 Zesty Zapus, the equivalent command with the iproute2 utilities would be:

ip route

Now that you know how to find your IP address, let's talk about how to actually obtain an IP address for your Ubuntu system.

Getting An Ip Address From Dhcp

Most of the time, your computer will receive an IP address from a DHCP server.

Configuring each individual computer with an IP address by hand is time-consuming and error prone; if one or more computers receive the same IP address, they won't be able to connect due to the address conflict. DHCP, which stands for "Dynamic Host Configuration Protocol", takes the guesswork out of the process. When a computer plugs into a Ethernet network (or connects to a wireless network), it sends out a request for a DHCP server. If there's a DHCP server on the network, it supplies the computer with an IP address, and the DHCP server ensures that no two computers receive the same IP address.

(We'll discuss the DHCP process in more detail in the next chapter.)

Most of the time, when you plug into a new network, you'll receive a DHCP address automatically. If you don't, however, try this command:

sudo dhclient

This will manually tell your system to search for a DHCP server and accept an address. If this command doesn't work, that means either the network you're using doesn't have a functioning DHCP server, or that something is blocking the DHCP server from communicating with your computer.

Releasing A Dhcp Address

DHCP addresses come with a "lease", which means the amount of time your computer is allowed to keep the address. Usually, your computer will contact the DHCP server at the halfway point before the lease expires, and ask for permission to keep it, which the DHCP server almost always grants.

Sometimes you want to release a leased IP address early - like if your network's DHCP server changes, or if your computer refuses to release its IP address. You can do this with the dhclient command and the -r option:

sudo dhclient -r

This releases your IP address, and you can then use sudo dhclient to contact a DHCP server to receive a new one.

Set A Static Ip From The Gui

DHCP address are convenient, but they have one big weakness - they can change quickly. If the lease length is short enough, your IP address could be 192.168.1.1 on Monday and 192.168.3.45 on Tuesday, depending on which addresses the DHCP server happens to have available. For laptop and desktop computers this normally isn't a big deal. Servers, however, need to have consistent IP addresses so client computers can locate them.

This is where a "static IP" address comes in. A static IP is one that you manually assign to a computer, one that it keeps forever or until you change it. You'll need to make sure that it doesn't conflict with your DHCP server, so you'll need to either reconfigure your DHCP server to exclude the static address from its address pool, or ask your system administrator to do it.

Here's how to set a static IP for your system's Ethernet adapter from the GUI.

-Launch Network Connections by clicking on the Dash and searching for it in the search field.

-When the Network Connections dialog box opens up, click on

the Wired tab, and then on the connection labeled etho. Click on the Edit button.

-When the Editing etho box opens up, click on the tab for IPv4 Settings.

-In the IPv4 box, change the Method drop-down box from Automatic to Manual.

-Under the Addresses heading, click the Add button to add a static IP, subnet mask, and default gateway.

-Add your DNS server to the DNS Servers line.

-Click OK.

This is kind of an involved procedure - I think it's easier to set a static address from the command line, which we'll cover in the next section.

Set A Static Ip

To set a static IP address from the command line in Ubuntu, you'll need to edit a pair of text files - specifically /etc/network/interfaces and /etc/resolv.conf. Time to break out those vi skills you learned in the last chapter! Only root has permission to edit the files in question, so you'll need to use sudo in conjunction with vi to make this work.

First, make a backup copy of the interfaces file:

sudo cp /etc/network/interfaces ~

This will make a backup copy in your home directory. Why make a backup copy? Before editing any configuration file in Ubuntu, it's always a good idea to make a backup copy in your home directory. That way, if something goes wrong, or you make a mistake, you can quickly restore the backup copy and get your system in working order again.

Next, open up the interfaces file in vi:

sudo vi /etc/network/interfaces

Initially, the file only contains information about your local loopback address. (The local loopback address is 127.0.0.1. It doesn't go anywhere, and it's used to test if your computer's TCP/IP stack is working properly):

auto lo

iface lo inet loopback

To give your system a static IP address, you'll need to make some changes to this file.

Let's say you want to assign a static IP of 192.168.1.2 to your eth0 network connection (which, as you'll recall, is the first adapter on your system - additional adapters will be numbered eth1, eth2, and so on), with a subnet mask of 255.255.255.0 and a local gateway of 192.168.1.1. Switch vi over to Insert mode and add the following lines:

auto eth0

iface eth0 inet static

address 192.168.1.2

netmask 255.255.255.0

broadcast 192.168.1.255

gateway 192.168.1.1

Once you've added these lines, enter Command mode in vi, and save and quit (you can do this with either the **qw** or the **exit** commands). You've added your static IP, subnet mask, and default gateway, but you'll still need to add a DNS server, and you can do that by editing the /etc/resolv.conf file:

sudo vi /etc/resolv.conf

To set a static DNS server with the address of 192.168.1.10, switch vi to Insert mode add this line to the file:

nameserver 192.168.1.10

Save the file, and exit your text editor.

You'll then to need have your system load the new IP configuration. You can do that by rebooting, but if that takes too long, you can use this command to force Ubuntu to re-read the configuration files:

sudo ifup eth0

Your system will then have a static IP address.

In the next chapter, we'll cover how to set up a DHCP Server.

Set A Static Dns Server Address

It is not immediately obvious how to set a static DNS server address from the command line in Ubuntu. In the Desktop version of Ubuntu, you can of course use the graphical Network Manager to assign a static DNS server. In the Server version, things are a little more complicated. In this section we will explain how to use the resolvconf utility to set a static address for the DNS server. (In this example, we will assume your DNS server has an address of 192.168.1.100.)

First, log into Ubuntu, and then navigate to this directory:

/etc/resolvconf/resolv.conf.d

Once you are in the appropriate directory, use this command to launch the vi text editor:

sudo vi /etc/resolvconf/resolv.conf.d/head

This will open up resolvconf's head text file in vi. Once vi has launched, press the INSERT key to switch vi to edit mode, and then enter the following line:

nameserver 192.168.1.100

Then hit the ESC key to switch vi back to command mode, and type this command to save the edited text file and then quit vi:

:wq

Once vi exits, type this command:

sudo resolvconf -u

The resolvconf utility will then read the head file and set the static DNS server address you entered.

8

BASIC FILE SHARING WITH SAMBA

One of the most common uses of a Ubuntu machine – whether a server or a desktop – is to share files across the network. If you're not familiar with the term, "file sharing" means to make a folder on your system available to clients on the network. From their own machines, users are able to access your shared folder from their computers, and depending upon how you've configured the security, they can copy the files for themselves, alter the files, add new files, or even delete files.

There are a number of different programs that offer file-sharing capabilities. Most Ubuntu systems use the "Samba" software, since it is can easily share files with Windows-based computers. It's common to find organizations that have a number of users with Windows systems storing their data on a Linux server running Samba.

What Is Samba?

Samba gets its name from the Server Message Block / Common Internet File System protocol, which is usually abbreviated to SMB/CIFS. A programmer named Andrew Tridgell first started developing what would become the Samba server in 1991 and 1992.

Initially he called the project "smbserver", but later he received a trademark notice from a company that owned the rights to that name. To find a different name, Tridgell searched the UNIX system dictionary for words containing the letters "s, m, b", and settled upon Samba.

Samba quickly became popular because it allowed easy file sharing between UNIX-based, and later Linux-based, computers and Windows systems. Today, Samba is widely used, and Windows, Mac OS X, and Linux clients can all access files on a Samba share.

We'll show you how to set up a basic Samba server, and how to access those shares from client computers.

Basic Samba Setup

Samba has a vast array of options and configuration settings, but here we'll show you how to set up and configure a basic Samba server with one user.

First, you'll need to install Samba. Make your way to a command prompt and type this command:

sudo apt-get install samba

Enter your password to authenticate, and **apt** will download and install Samba and its attendant utilities for you.

In Chapter 3 we talked about Ubuntu's user accounts, noting that they're stored in the /etc/passwd file. A key thing to understand about Samba is that it stores its own set of user accounts, separate from the main accounts, in the /etc/samba/smbpasswd file. That means you'll need to create a separate Samba password for every user you want to access your file shares. You create this password using the **smbpasswd** command. Using the camalas account for Caina Amalas that we created in Chapter 5, here's how the command should look:

sudo smbpasswd -a camalas

Be sure to give camalas's Samba account an appropriately strong password (including uppercase, lowercase, punctuation, and numbers). Once camalas's password is created, the next step is to create a directory for her to share. Begin by creating a folder named 'test' in camalas's folder, which we'll use for our first shared folder:

mkdir /home/camalas/test

(NOTE: *DO NOT* use sudo to create the folder, because then the owning user and group will be set as 'root', which means you won't be able to access the folder using your Samba username and password.)

The next step is to edit the /etc/samba/smb.conf file, the main configuration file for Samba. As always, make a safe backup copy of the original smb.conf file to your home folder, in case you make an error:

sudo cp /etc/samba/smb.conf ~

Now use vi to edit the /etc/samba/smb.conf file:

sudo vi /etc/samba/smb.conf

The smb.conf file is long and rather complex, but for the purposes of this demonstration, you can ignore most of it. Key down to the very end of the file and insert this text:

[test]
path = /home/camalas/test
available = yes
valid users = camalas
read only = no
browseable = yes
public = yes
writable = yes

(There should be no spaces between the lines, and note also that there should be a single space both before and after each of the equal signs.)

Here's what some of the more important configuration options mean.

-The "[test]" gives the name of the file share.

-The "path" option specifies the location of the folder to be shared.

-The "available" option specifies that the file share is available to clients on the network.

-The "valid users" option details the users that are allowed to access the file share. In this case, we've set it so that only the camalas account can access it. You can add additional accounts here, if you prefer.

-The "read only" option specifies whether nor not clients will be allowed to write to the file share.

-The "writable" option specifies that data can be written to the file share.

The settings specified above will share the test folder we created earlier, and give the camalas username and the camalas username alone permission to read and write to the folder. Once you have input the changes, save smb.conf, exit vi, and restart Samba with this command:

sudo /etc/init.d/smbd restart

(This will force Samba to restart, re-reading its configuration files and activating the share you just created.)

Once Samba has restarted, use this command to check your smb.-conf for any syntax errors:

sudo testparm

If you pass the testparm command, Samba should be working. Try accessing the share from another client on your LAN.

We'll explain how to do that before the end of the chapter.

Accessing Shared Folders From A Ubuntu Client

If you followed the directions in the previous section, you should have a working Samba server on your Ubuntu system.

Accessing the file share from another Ubuntu system is simple enough, using the GUI. To access the share from a client Ubuntu system, launch Nautilus File Explorer, and then click on the Other Locations item in the Sidebar. When the Other Locations window appears, enter your Samba server's IP address into the Connect To Server field, and hit Connect. An icon for the server should then appear in the Sidebar. Double-click the icon, and you'll be asked for a username and password. Put in the username and password of the account that has access to share, and you should have access to it.

To access the file shares from a command-line client takes a little more work.

First, you'll need to install the **cifs-utils** and the **smbfs** packages on the client system. Go to a command prompt and type this command:

sudo apt-get install cifs-utils smbclient

Enter your password to authenticate, and **apt** will download and install those packages for you. Once the packages are installed, you can use them to connect to a Samba server.

Now, to continue our previous example, let's say that you followed all the walkthroughs in the previous chapter, which means you have a Ubuntu server running Samba with an IP address of 192.168.1.2, hosting a shared folder called "test". You created the camalas account, and let's say you assigned that account a password of "ghost". You want to access that file share from a client computer.

First, query the Samba server to see what shares are available with this command:

sudo smbclient -L 192.168.1.2

This will display a list of any shares available on the Samba server. You should see the test share available.

Now let's say you actually want to connect to the "test" share on 192.168.1.1. First, you'll need a "mount point", a place in your client computer's filesystem where it can mount the Samba share as a directory. If you don't already have a mount point, you can make one with this command:

mkdir ~/mount

This will generate a directory called mount in your home folder. We'll use it in the next command to mount the Samba share.

To actually mount the Samba share, use this command:

sudo mount //192.168.1.2/test ~/mount -o username=camalas,password=ghost

This will mount the shared directory "test" on 192.168.1.1 in the "mount" folder we just created in the client's home directory.

To unmount the shared folder, simply use this command:

sudo umount ~/mount

This will dismount the file share from your client computer.

Note that the command is in fact actually spelled "umount", not "unmount" – accidentally typing "unmount" for the **umount** command is a common typographical mistake.

Accessing Shared Folders From A Windows Client

Generally, connecting to a Samba share on Ubuntu machine from a Windows client should be straightforward. However, there are a few pitfalls to beware.

Let's assume that you've stuck with the settings we've used already, and you now have a Ubuntu Samba server with an IP address of 192.168.1.2 (and a subnet mask of 255.255.255.0). The server hosts a share called "test", and the user account "camalas" has access with a password of "ghost." You want to connect to this share from a Windows machine with an IP of 192.168.1.3 and a subnet mask of 255.255.255.0.

On the Windows machine, go to Start menu, and then to Run (or hit the Windows Key and R simultaneously), and type this into the Run box:

\\192.168.1.2

Alternately, you can also type this into the address bar in any Windows Explorer window. This is what's called an UNC path - a "Universal Naming Convention" path.

Unless you have a DNS server set up, it's better to use the IP address instead of the hostname to access your Ubuntu machine from Windows. In fact, if you don't have a DNS server set up, you'll *have* to use the IP address to get to the Samba server from your Windows machine, since your Windows machine won't be able to resolve the Ubuntu's IP address. Giving your Ubuntu machine a static IP address, as we discussed in Chapter 7, would make this easier.

Click OK if you typed the UNC into the Run box, or hit the Enter key if you typed it into Windows Explorer, and you should receive a username and password prompt for the share. Using the example above, enter your username and password in this format:

camalas@192.168.1.2

ghost

It's necessary to enter the username as "**camalas@192.168.1.2**" (or as **192.168.1.2\camalas**, alternately), because otherwise Windows tries to authenticate the Samba share against its own accounts. That, of course, will not work. Using the IP address in the account name forces Windows to authenticate against the Samba server.

If that doesn't work, first make sure you've typed the username, the password, and the IP address correctly. One mistake and it won't work, and the password IS case sensitive. Next, check the /etc/samba/smb.conf file to make sure the share permissions are set correctly. Also check the filesystem permissions and ownership of the folder you are trying to access. Your user account will need to have permission to actually get at the share folder, regardless of the share permissions. If you created the share folder using sudo, for instance, the root user and the root group will have ownership of the folder, and you won't be able to get at it using your Samba account.

9

FTP CLIENT AND SERVER

F TP stands for "file transfer protocol", and it allows you to transfer files to a remote computer. FTP has been around forever, and it has a number of pros and cons. Since FTP is so old, it is supported on virtually every operating system, and most operating systems include an FTP client of some kind. The downside is that FTP is not terribly secure. It has a bad habit of rotating ports, which makes it hard to use across the Internet (firewalls really don't like having ports change on them abruptly), and an FTP server that allows for anonymous login is tremendously insecure - anyone can upload or download material, which means that an FTP server that allows anonymous access can quickly find itself hosting illegal material. (These days, FTP servers that allow anonymous access are quite extremely rare.) I strongly prefer to use SFTP instead, which we will discuss in Chapter II.

However, Ubuntu can act as an FTP server with a reasonable degree of security. In this chapter, we'll show you how to set up Ubuntu as an FTP server, and how to use a command-line FTP client.

Install And Configure An Ftp Server

The most common FTP server software for Ubuntu is the vsftpd package, which stands for "very secure FTP daemon." It's the default FTP package for Ubuntu, and most other Linux distributions as well. As an added bonus, vsftpd is pretty secure out of the box - to make it insecure, you have to go out of your way to mess up the configuration file.

As an added bonus, vsftpd is simple to install and configure on a Ubuntu machine. To install the vsftpd package, make your way to a command prompt and type this command:

sudo apt-get install vsftpd

Enter your password to authenticate and **apt** will download and install vsftpd for you.

Follow the default prompts, and the vsftpd server will be installed on your computer. Generally, the default configuration for vsftpd is pretty secure, and good enough for casual use. Anonymous users are blocked, and no one can write files to the server (or, in FTP terminology, no one can upload files to the server). Anyone with a system account will be able to connect to the FTP server and download, though not upload, files.

If you want to change any settings, the configuration file for vsftpd is /etc/vsftpd.conf. Like any other configuration file, you can edit it with vi:

sudo vi /etc/vsftpd.conf

Like Samba, the vsftpd.conf file contains a large number of "directives" that govern how the server behaves and operates. If you want to change its configuration, you'll need to alter the directives.

If you want users to be able to write files to your FTP server, change this directive:

#write_enable=YES

To this:

write_enable=YES

With the write_enable directive set to YES, users will be able to upload files to your FTP server. Note, however, that they will only be able to do so if they have proper permissions to the directories in question. They'll be able to upload files to their home directories, but not, for instance /var or /usr.

Anonymous access is controlled with this directive:

anonymous_enable=NO

Under no circumstances should you allow anonymous access to your FTP server, especially if it is accessible from the Internet! There are certain circumstances when you might find it useful, but you should only enable it if you know *exactly* what you are doing. Generally, it is almost always best to keep **anonymous_enable** set to NO.

If you make any changes to the file, switch vi to command mode, save the changes, and then exit vi. Then restart the vsftpd server so it reads its new directives:

sudo service vsftpd restart

You can then test your Ubuntu machine's FTP service from the server's command line:

ftp 127.0.0.1

The FTP client will ask for your username. Enter that, and then the client will ask for your password. Enter that as well, and you should then see the FTP prompt, which looks like this:

ftp>

If you see that, you know the server is working. You can return to the regular command line with this command:

exit

Using The Ftp Client

Just because you have an FTP server doesn't mean you can access it straightaway - you first need a program called an "FTP client" that will let you communicate with the FTP server. Fortunately, Ubuntu comes with a built-in FTP client - you can access it from the command line by simply typing:

ftp

However, it's far easier to use if you know the IP address of the FTP server you want to access. Let's say you want to access a FTP server with an IP address of 192.168.1.100. To do so, you would append the IP address to the ftp client command:

ftp 192.168.1.100

The FTP client will then ask for your username. (Note that this will be your username and password on the FTP server, not your username and password on the computer with the FTP client.) Type it and hit enter. The client will ask for your password, which you should then enter. Once you do, you'll be taken to the FTP prompt, which looks like this:

ftp>

You can also specify a different username as part of the ftp command. If, for instance, you wanted to use our camalas account to connect to the FTP server at 192.168.1.100, the command would look like this:

ftp camalas@192.168.1.100

Once at the FTP prompt, you can use some of the common terminal commands. To see a listing of the remote directory, you can use the ls command:

ls

This will display the contents of the remote directory.

To find which remote directory you're actually in, you can use the pwd command:

pwd

This command, as you might remember from Chapter 1, stands for "print working directory", and will display the current working directory.

To download files from the FTP server, you will need to use the **get** command. For instance, to retrieve a file named "report.doc" from the current working directory:

get report.doc

This will download the file to your local home directory.

To upload files to the FTP server (assuming that the server's write_enable directive is set to YES), you'll need to use the **put** command. To put a file named "data.doc" on the remote server:

put data.doc

This will upload the file to the remote directory on the FTP server.

This is only a basic overview of the commands available with the FTP client - many more are available. Also, if you would prefer to use a graphical FTP client, I would recommend the excellent Filezilla client, which you can install with this command:

sudo apt-get install filezilla

10

USING SSH AND SFTP

S SH stands for "secure shell", and it is a network protocol that allows you to securely send commands to a remote machine. We discussed in Chapter 1 how a "shell" is a program that provides an interface between the user and the operating system. SSH is a "remote" shell that allows you to send commands to a machine over the network. The "secure" part comes from the fact that the connection is encrypted, which means that an attacker cannot eavesdrop on the connection, or intercept and replace your commands with his own midway through transit. SSH is pretty reliable and secure, and is commonly used in the Linux world. Administrators often use it to remotely manage machines – it's usually more comfortable to control a server from your laptop than in the chilly and noisy server room.

SSH also offers the SFTP protocol, which stands for "SSH File Transfer Protocol". Basically, SFTP is similar to the FTP protocol, but it uses SSH's security functions to encrypt the connection. That means SFTP is much more secure than FTP.

In this chapter, we'll show you how to set up an SSH server, how to use the SSH command-line client, and how to use SFTP. We'll also show you how to set up SSH to use key-based authentication, which is much more secure than password-based authentication.

Install And Configure An Ssh Server

Linux has always had strong support for SSH, and Ubuntu is no different. In this section, we'll walk through a basic installation of an SSH server, and some basic security configuration as well. The default SSH server package for Ubuntu is OpenSSH Server, which we'll use here.

First, you'll need to install OpenSSH Server. To do so, open up a Terminal window and type the following command:

sudo apt-get install openssh-server

Enter your password to authenticate, and the **apt** utility will download and install OpenSSH Server for you. Depending on the speed of your Internet connection and your computer, the installation may take several minutes.

Once the installation has finished, return to the Terminal window. We'll need to make a few changes to your /etc/ssh/sshd_config file in order to increase SSH's security. First, as always, we'll want to make a backup copy of your sshd_config file in case anything goes wrong. Type this command into the Terminal:

sudo cp /etc/ssh/sshd_config ~

This will make a backup copy of the sshd_config file in your home directory.

Next, we'll need to edit the sshd_config file itself. So it's time to use your skills in vi again:

sudo vi /etc/ssh/sshd_config

Like almost every other server software package, SSH is controlled by a number of directives in its configuration file. The default installation of OpenSSH server is reasonably secure. However, you might want to make a few changes to tighten up its security to additional degree.

The "PermitRootLogin" directive is one you'll want to change.

Once you're editing the /etc/ssh/sshd_config file, you'll want to change the following directive as follows:

PermitRootLogin no

This will keep anyone from attempting to log into your server via SSH as root. It's generally a good idea not to allow any to log into your SSH server as root. If an attacker manages to hack into your SSH server with the root login, he will have complete control over your machine, and that is definitely not a good thing.

Another directive you might want to change is the "AllowUsers." When the AllowUsers directive is active, only users specifically specified in the directive can access the system through SSH. This adds an additional layer of protection to your SSH server by only allowing specific users to connect via SSH. For instance, if you wanted to limit SSH access to just the "camalas" user account, edit the AllowUsers directive like this:

AllowUsers camalas

To add multiple users to the AllowUsers directive, just add them one by one without commas or semicolons. An AllowUsers directive that permits the camalas user account and the lmaraeus user account to log in would look like this:

AllowUsers camalas lmaraeus

You may also want to consider changing the Port directive. By default SSH runs over TCP/IP port 22, which means that any malware bot autoscanning port 22 can target it. If you set up your user accounts with a weak password (always a bad idea), eventually an automated bot might break through and guess the password. Changing the Port directive to something different will make SSH run over a different port, blocking some of those automated cracking attempts. To set SSH to run over port 5699 instead, make sure your Port directive looks like this:

Port 5699

Note that if you change your SSH server's default port, you'll need to remember the new port number when using an SSH client, which we'll cover in the next section.

After you've finished changing the directives in /etc/ssh/sshd_config, switch vi to command mode, and save and quit vi. After you return to the command line, restart the SSH daemon with this command:

sudo /etc/init.d/ssh restart

You should now be able to SSH into your Ubuntu machine from another system with an SSH client.

Configure Ssh To Use Key-Based Authentication

SSH is pretty secure, but it does have one weak link – the password. If someone cracks your SSH password, they can gain control over your SSH server.

A more secure method of SSH logons is to use a public/private key. With a public/private key, you create a matched pair of private and public keys. You keep the private key on your personal machine, while you put the public key on the SSH server to which you wish to connect. When configured in this manner, the SSH server will only allow connections from systems that have a matching private key for one of the public keys.

In this section, we'll show you how to set up key-based logons for SSH.

First, install OpenSSH server on your server. For the rest of this walkthrough, we'll assume that you installed the SSH server on a machine with the IP address of 192.168.1.100, and that you intend to connect to that server from a client machine with the IP address of 192.168.1.200.

After SSH server has been installed, go to your client machine at 192.168.1.200 and enter this command:

ssh-keygen -t dsa

Press Enter, and the command will save a matched public/private key in the ~/.sshdirectory. Specifically, it creates two files – id_dsa, which is your private key, andid_dsa.pub, which is your public key. It will also ask you to set a passphrase for the use of the key, which is an additional layer of security in case someone gains access to your account. Setting a passphrase is usually a good idea.

After the command is complete, you'll need to transfer the newly created id_dsa.pubpublic key file to your SSH server at 192.168.1.100. Once you have moved it to your server, copy the file to your user account's ~/.ssh directory on the server. (If this directory does not already exist, create it with the mkdir command.) Next, change to the~/.ssh directory, and use this command:

touch authorized_keys

This will create a file to store authorized keys in the ~/.ssh directory. Use this command to add your public key to the authorized_keys file:

cat id_dsa.pub >> authorized_keys

Finally, use the chmod command to make authorized_keys read-only to protect from accidental deletion:

chmod 400 authorized_keys

Finally, you'll need to alter your SSH server's configuration file to mandate key-based logins, otherwise the server will continue to allow password-based login. Use the vi editor to edit SSH's main configuration file:

sudo vi /etc/ssh/sshd_config

Once editing the file, make sure the PasswordAuthentication directive is set to no. This will force your SSH server to only allow key-based login attempts. After you've finished editing the file, restart your SSH server with this command:

sudo service ssh restart

Your SSH server will not only permit key-based logons – users must have a private key that matches with a corresponding public key in their ~/.ssh/authorized_keys file in their home folder on the SSH server.

Make sure to back up your private key in a safe place – if you lose it, you will lose access to the SSH server.

Using An Ssh Client

Almost all Linux distributions, including Ubuntu, come with a command-line SSH client. Once you successfully connect to an SSH server, it's as if you were sitting front of that machine, using a command line session. You can issue commands, move and delete files, and run programs, limited only by your permissions on the SSH server.

Let's say you want to connect to an SSH server with the IP address of 192.168.1.100. To do so, you would simply use the ssh command at the command line to launch the SSH client:

ssh 192.168.1.100

The first time you connect to a new SSH server, the client will display the server's RSA fingerprint (RSA is a kind of encryption), and will ask if you want to continue connecting. Type out "yes" and hit enter (just hitting "y" won't work). The SSH client will then ask for a username and password, and assuming you type those correctly, you'll be in. You can then start using the remote machine as if you were sitting in front of it.

However, you might want to skip a step. With the addition of the – l switch, you can specify a username with the ssh command. In this example, the SSH client will attempt to connect using the "camalas" username:

ssh –l camalas 192.168.1.100

You'll only need to enter the password for camalas's account to connect.

By default, the SSH client attempts to connect using Port 22. However, if you used the Port directive in your SSH server's /etc/ssh/sshd_config file to change the default port, your SSH client won't be able to connect, and will come back with an error message. In our example above, we set the SSH server to listen on the 5699 port. To tell the SSH client to connect using that port, use the –p switch:

ssh –p 5589 192.168.1.100

You can also combine that with the –l switch as well:

ssh –p 5589 –l camalas 192.168.1.100

This will make the ssh client attempt to create an ssh connection to 192.168.1.100 using port 5589 and the camalas user account.

Using Sftp

SFTP, as mentioned above, is basically the File Transfer Protocol run over an SSH connection. Since it uses SSH's encryption, it's much more secure than traditional FTP. As an added bonus, there's no need to set up a separate SFTP server – the OpenSSH Server package includes a built in SFTP server, which is also governed by the /etc/ssh/sshd_config file. Like with an FTP server, you need an SFTP client – but Ubuntu (and most Linux distributions) include one by default.

You can access the SFTP client from the command line by simply typing:

sftp

However, it's far easier to use if you know the IP address of the SSH server you want to access. Let's say you want to access a SSH server with an IP address of 192.168.1.100. To do so, you would append the IP address to the sftp client command:

sftp 192.168.1.100

The SSH client will then ask for your username. (Note that this will be your username and password on the SSH server, not the computer with the SFTP client.) Type it and hit enter. The client will ask for your password, which you should then enter. Once you do, you'll be taken to the SFTP prompt, which looks like this:

sftp>

You can also specify a different username as part of the **sftp** command. If, for instance, you wanted to use our camalas account to connect to the SSH server at 192.168.1.100, the command would look like this:

sftp camalas@192.168.1.100

If you set up the SSH server to listen on a different port than the default of port 22, you'll need to tell the SFTP client to use a different port with the "-P" switch. Note that this is different than the SSH client, which uses the "-p" switch – remember that the Linux command line is case-sensitive. To make the SFTP client use the 5589 port, the command should look like this:

sftp −P 5589 192.168.1.100

Once at the sftp prompt, you can use some of the common terminal commands. To see a listing of the remote directory, you can use the ls command:

ls

This will display the contents of the remote directory.

To find which remote directory you're actually in, you can use the pwd command:

pwd

This command, as you might remember from Chapter 1, stands for "print working directory", and will display the current working directory.

To download files from the SSH server, you will need to use the **get** command. For instance, to retrieve a file named "report.doc" from the current working directory:

get report.doc

This will download the file to your local home directory.

To upload files to the SSH server, you'll need to use the **put** command. To put a file named "data.doc" on the remote server:

put data.doc

This will upload the file to the remote directory on the SSH server.

THE SSH CLIENT ON WINDOWS AND MACINTOSH MACHINES

NOW THAT YOU have your Ubuntu machine set up as an SSH server, you might want to know if you can connect to it from a Windows or a Macintosh system.

The answer is yes! The Mac, in particular, makes it easy. Mac OS X is a version of UNIX, and if you remember the introduction, Linux and UNIX are closely related. The Mac has both a built-in SSH client and an SFTP client which you can use from the Mac OS X Terminal utility. (Terminal is the Utilities folder in the Mac's Applications folder.) Additionally, you can also set up a Mac machine as an SSH server. If you go to System Preferences, and then the Sharing control panel, you can check "Remote Login" to enable the Mac to act as an SSH server. From the Sharing control panel, you can also select the users allowed to SSH into the Mac.

Windows comes with no-built in SSH capability. However, a number of SSH clients are available for the Windows platform. My favorite is the PuTTY client, which can act as both a Telnet and an SSH client. If you need an SFTP client for Windows, the redoubtable graphical program FileZilla (which we mentioned with Ubuntu's FTP server) can act as an SFTP client, and it's available for Windows.

11

INSTALL AND CONFIGURE APACHE WEB SERVER

F or both good and for evil, the Internet has revolutionized how people communicate, buy goods and services, read books, listen to music, and find friends and potential spouses. The very existence of this book is a testament to the power of the Internet – after all, you probably bought this book from a site selling eBooks, and the Ubuntu install disc is downloaded over the Internet. In point of fact, this book only exists at all because of the Internet – almost certainly no paper publisher would put out a short introductory book on Ubuntu (let alone one written by a fantasy author!).

At the heart of the Internet revolution is a piece of software called a web server. What a web server does is host HTML documents called web pages, which are then served up to client web browsers across the World Wide Web. Web pages can range from simple static HTML pages to elaborate web apps providing banking, commerce, and social networking functions.

Linux might not have the desktop share of Microsoft Windows, but it dominates the web server market. Between 33 to 40 percent (depending on who's doing the counting) of web servers are Linux/UNIX/UNIX-like machines running a program called Apache

HTTP Server, most commonly referred to as just "Apache." Apache has been around since 1995 or so, and its development has fueled the growth of the World Wide Web.

You can easily install Apache on a Ubuntu system. A Ubuntu machine can serve as a web server for simple static HTML pages, and can scale up to supporting large and complex web applications. In this chapter, we'll show you how to set up a simple Apache server. In later chapters, we'll build on that install to run some more powerful web applications, like WordPress and MediaWiki.

Install Apache Web Server

As installations go, installing Apache on Ubuntu is a breeze. (Configuring it, of course, is substantially more difficult.) To install Apache, type this command at a Terminal window or a command prompt:

sudo apt-get install apache2

(Technically, you'll be installing Apache 2, the latest version.)

Enter your password to authenticate, follow the default prompts, and apt will download and install the Apache web server for you.

And that's it! Apache should now be working. To test it from the web server itself, go to a web browser and visit the address http://127.0.0.1. You'll remember that this is the "local loopback" address, basically the IP address the local computer uses to refer to itself. Alternatively, you could test it from another computer on the same subnet. For instance, if you installed Apache on a computer with an IP address of 192.168.1.100, you could test it by going to another computer on the same subnet and visiting http://192.168.100 from the web browser.

Regardless, if Apache is working properly, you should see the default Apache/Ubuntu web page with the Ubuntu logo in the upper left-hand corner.

Apache is now operational. In the next section we'll talk a little bit about configuring Apache.

Basic Apache Configuration

Apache configuration can get extremely complex, depending on the scale of the website involved. A full overview of Apache configuration is way beyond the scope of this book – indeed, dozens of excellent books have been written on the topic. However, here we can take a brief look at Apache configuration.

Apache's chief configuration file is /etc/apache2/apache2.conf. (In some Linux distributions, it's /etc/apache2/httpd.conf, but Ubuntu uses /etc/apache2/apache2.conf.) You can look around in the file using **vi**, **cat**, or **less**, but it's generally a good idea to change things only if you know what you're doing. And as always, make sure to create a backup copy of a configuration file in your home directory before you alter it, in case something goes irretrievably wrong.

Ubuntu stores your actual web files (the HTML files that make up your website) in the /var/www/html directory. After an installation of Apache, there's only one file in that directory – the index.html file, which contains the "it works!" message we saw earlier. Otherwise the directory is empty. You can put your own HTML files in here. Coding HTML is beyond the scope of this book, but remember that you'll need to create your own index.html file once you build your own site.

However, loading HTML files into the /var/www/html directory will only allow you to create a static website. If you want a dymanic website, once that updates content, you'll need a database backend – and we'll discuss that in the next chapter. In the next section of this chapter, we'll show you how to set up Apache to use virtual hosts.

Virtual Hosts

As we've discussed in the previous section, it is easy to set up a simple web server with Apache. However, you might need a more complex web server, one that can host multiple separate websites, rather than subdirectories within a larger website.

. . .

How do you do this?

Apache has a feature called "virtual hosts" that lets you run separate websites, with completely different domain names, on the same physical server. Fortunately, implementing virtual hosts for Apache is actually quite simple to do. In this example, we'll show you how to set up a new website called "examplename.com" on an Apache web server.

First, you'll need to set a location for your new web site's files. Apache, you might recall, by default stores the web files in /var/www/html. For this example, create a new folder for the website with this command:

sudo mkdir /var/www/html/w2

Next, you'll need to create a configuration file for the new website in the /etc/apache2/sites-available directory. Fortunately, that directory contains a default file you can simply copy and use as a template with this command:

sudo   cp   /etc/apache2/sites-available/000-default.conf /etc/apache2/sites-available/examplename.conf

(Make sure to include .conf extension. Ubuntu 14.04 Trusty Tahr and above run Apache 2.4, which requires it.)

The next step is to edit the new configuration file with the correct settings. You can do this using the **vi** text editor:

sudo vi /etc/apache2/sites-available/examplename.conf

(We discussed how to use **vi** back in Chapter 6.)

Once editing the file with **vi**, you'll need to make a few changes.

Change the "Document Root" directive from /var/www/html to the proper location of your new website, in this case, /var/www/html/w2.

Also change the "Directory" directive from /var/www/html to /var/www/html/w2.

Finally, under the line that begins "ServerAdmin", add a new line for the new website's domain name. For our website named "examplename.com", add a line like this:

ServerName examplename.com

Save changes to the configuration file, and then exit **vi.**

Now you'll need to modify Apache to display the new domain names to web visitors. Fortunately, you can do this with the a2ensite command:

sudo a2ensite examplename.conf

(Note that "examplename" would change depending upon what you named your configuration file.)

One final step – restart Apache to force it to re-read its configuration files and start serving the new website:

sudo /etc/init/d apache2 restart

Make sure you have some sort of index.html file in /var/www/html/w2, and the examplename.com website should now be working.

12

INSTALL AND CONFIGURE MYSQL SERVER AND PHPMYADMIN

Y ou've probably heard the term "database" thrown around, but may or may not have a clear idea what it means. Put simply, a database is any system designed to create, store, retrieve, and manage a large amount of digital information. There are many different kinds of databases, but the most common kind is a "relational database", a database that uses multiple tables (and each table has many rows and columns) to store the necessary data. Most modern databases are technically a RDBMS, a "relational database management system", which is a way of describing a database (and any attendant software) that uses the relational model.

The most popular and widely-used open-source RDBMS currently in use is a program called MySQL. Two computer programmers named Michael Widenius and David Axmark began developing MySQL in 1994, and the software was eventually acquired by Sun Corporation, and then by Oracle Corporation, when Oracle bought Sun in 2010. The name "MySQL" comes from two sources. The "My" part apparently comes from Michael Widenius's daughter, named My. The "SQL" comes from "Structured Query Language", which is a computer language designed to handle the tasks of inserting, retrieving, managing, and deleting data in an RDBMS.

MySQL has been around for a long time, and it's used in a lot of websites – Google, Facebook, and Wikipedia all use MySQL, and many of the more popular content management systems, like Word-Press and Drupal, rely on MySQL to store data.

MySQL installs quite easily on a Ubuntu system. In this chapter, we'll show you how to install and configure MySQL, how to create databases and database users from the MySQL command line, and how to install phpMyAdmin for an easier, graphical-based means of configuring MySQL

Install Mysql Server

To install MySQL Server on Ubuntu, make your way to a Terminal window or a command prompt, and type this command:

sudo apt-get install mysql-server-5.7

(As of this writing, MySQL Server version 5.7 is the latest version available in the Ubuntu repositories, though future versions of Ubuntu may receive the newer versions of MySQL.)

Enter your password to authenticate, and apt will download the MySQL files and install them for you. It's a big set of files, so depending on the speed of your Internet connection, it might take a while to download. After the files are downloaded and are installing, the installer will ask you for a password for MySQL's root user. Just as the root user in Linux has complete control over the system, the root user in MySQL has absolute control over all databases, tables, permissions, and users. For obvious security reasons, you'll want to create an extremely strong password (a mixture of uppercase, lowercase, numbers, and punctuation, the longer the better) for your MySQL root user.

(Note that in the password dialog box, if you can't get the <OK> field selected, you can use the tab key to jump from the text input line to the <OK> field.)

Note also that as of Ubuntu 18.04, a root password is no longer set for MySQL, but instead the system's root user serves as the MySQL root user, so you access the MySQL command line client using the sudo command.

After you enter the root password, the installer will finish working with the MySQL files, and return you to the command line.

Next, you'll want to run the mysql_secure_installation script to tighten up security on your new MySQL server. Run this command from the prompt:

sudo mysql_secure_installation

First, the mysql_secure_installation script will ask you to enter the current password for the MySQL root user. After you do that, it will ask if you want to change the root password. Since you already set a root password, you can hit "n" (unless you want to change it again for some reason).

Next, the script will ask you to setup the VALIDATE PASSWORD plugin, which checks passwords for appropriate strength. Hit Y to accept, and then set the password strength level by hitting 0 for Low, 1, for Medium, and 2 for Strong.

Next, the script will ask if you want to remove the anonymous user. The anonymous user, like anonymous access in FTP, lets someone log into MySQL without having a proper user account. For security reasons, it's always best to remove the anonymous user, so hit "y" to continue.

After that, the script will ask if you want to prevent the MySQL root user from logging in remotely to the MySQL server. Always hit "y" to forbid root remote access, since if an attacker guesses your root password, he can destroy your databases or steal the information they contain.

After this, the script will ask if you want to remove the test database. MySQL includes a test database that anyone can access. Again, this is a security hole, so you'll want to hit "y" to remove the test database.

The script will then ask to reload the privilege tables so the changes take effect. Hit "y", and the **mysql_secure_installation** script will conclude and return you to the command line.

MySQL server is now installed on your Ubuntu system. In the

next section, we'll discuss using the MySQL command-line client to create databases and users.

Using The Mysql Command-Line Client

The most common use for MySQL on a Ubuntu system is to provide a backend for a dynamic website of some kind, usually content management systems like WordPress or MediaWiki. To host these websites on a Ubuntu machine, you'll need to create a database and a database user for the website. MySQL Server can support many different databases, limited by the amount of hardware and disk space available on the machine. (Hosting multiple active databases at the same time places a high level of demand upon a hard drive.)

Like Samba, MySQL has its own collection of user accounts, separate from the main system accounts, called "database users." A database user is simply a MySQL user that has access to a particular database, or specific tables within a database. In this section, we'll show you how to create database and users with the command-line client.

First, you'll need to get to the MySQL client prompt. The MySQL command-line client, like the command-line clients for FTP and SFTP, has its own prompt. To access that prompt and start the client on Ubuntu 17.10 and earlier, use this command:

mysql

However, if you simply type the command, it will bounce back with an error message. To use the MySQL command-line client, you need to add the -u and the -p switches as well. The -u switch tells it what MySQL user you want to use to log into the client (similar to the -l switch with SSH). The -p switch tells it to ask for the password. So, to use the MySQL client as the MySQL root user, the command should look like this:

mysql -u root -p

Enter the password for the MySQL root user, and you'll find yourself at the MySQL command prompt, which will look like this:

mysql>

If you are using MySQL on Ubuntu 18.04 and above, you will need to use the sudo command to launch the MySQL command line client:

sudo mysql

Enter your password, and if your account has administrative rights to your system, you will then enter the MySQL client.

Our next steps are to create a database, create a user to access that database, and grant our new user all rights to that database. Generally, when you're installing a web application like WordPress, you'll give the database user you create for the WordPress application all rights to the WordPress database so it can function properly. Not giving the application user all rights to the database can cause the application to act erratically or even fail entirely (though some applications can work with limited access to its database).

An important note before we continue, though. All commands made from the MySQL prompt must end with a semicolon to denote the end of the statement. Any commands that do not end with a semicolon will not work. With that in mind, let's first create a database.

To create a database, use this command at the **mysql>** prompt:

CREATE DATABASE newdatabase;

The MySQL client will respond with a message that should say "Query OK, 1 row affect (0.00 sec)." This means the command was successful, and a new database named "newdatabase" has been created.

Next, you'll create a user who will access that database:

CREATE USER newdatabaseruser;

You should get the "Query OK" message again. Once the new user is created, we'll need to set a password for the user before we can assign any permissions. In this example, we'll assign a password of "1234". However, in real life, just as with the root user, you'll want to assign a strong password. (This database user won't have full control over the MySQL server as the root user does, but we will give it full control over the database we just created, and a malicious user who guesses the password could cause all kinds of trouble.) To create the password, use this command:

SET PASSWORD FOR newdatabaseuser= PASSWORD("1234");

Again you should get the "Query OK" confirmation message. The final step is to assign all privileges on the "newdatabase" database to the "newdatabaseuser" user. Use this command to assign the permissions:

GRANT ALL PRIVILEGES ON newdatabase.* TO newdata-baseuser IDENTIFIED BY '1234;

That isn't a typo - those are single quote marks (') instead of the usual double quote marks (") that were used in the command to set the password. MySQL's internal syntax, alas, isn't always consistent. Anyway, if you typed the command correctly, you should get the "Query OK" confirmation again.

Once you are done, use this command to quit the MySQL command-line interface:

exit

You've now set up a database, created a database user, and given that user full control over that database.

Back Up And Restore Mysql Databases

MySQL databases are often used to power web applications such as WordPress or Moodle, which means that those MySQL databases often wind up holding vital information. Therefore, it is important to back them up on a regular basis. A quick and easy way to backup a MySQL database is with the mysqldump command-line tool. This tool downloads the database into a single SQL file, which you can store as a backup or use to transfer the database to another MySQL server.

To use mysqldump, you will need to know the root password of the MySQL server (or a user with permissions to the database you need to download).

In this example, we will dump a database named data into a file named data.sql:

mysqldump -u root -p data > data.sql

Enter the root password, and mysqldump will dump the database information into the data.sql file.

To transfer the database to a new server, first create a blank database on the server from the MySQL command prompt. In this example, this command will create a new database named datanew:

CREATE DATABASE datanew;

Then transfer the data.sql file to the new server and write it onto the new database with this command:

mysql -u root -p datanew < data.sql

The datanew database will receive all the tables and columns contained in the data.sql file. Note that this command completely overwrites the target database with the information in the SQL file, so make sure to select the correct database!

Installing Phpmyadmin

It is possible to administer MySQL Server entirely from its command line client.

But if you read through the previous section, you probably noticed that the MySQL command-line client is a lot of work, and rather cumbersome to boot. Remembering the syntax is something of a challenge, and occasionally even veteran database administrators have a hard time working through complex SQL statements. I am a big believer in doing as much as possible from the command line, but sometimes the GUI is in fact quicker and easier. MySQL administration is often one of those cases.

Fortunately, MySQL has a GUI available, a program called phpMyAdmin. It's a web interface, which means that you connect to it via a web browser from another computer. It runs off the PHP scripting language (which we'll discuss more in the next chapter), and lets you quickly and efficiently make changes to your MySQL Server. It even lets you enter command-line SQL statements, if you prefer.

Obviously, you will need MySQL Server installed before you can install phpMyAdmin. Once you have MySQL installed, you're ready to begin.

To install phpMyAdmin, go to a Terminal window or command prompt and type this command:

sudo apt-get install phpmyadmin

This will download and install phpMyAdmin on your Ubuntu system. The phpMyAdmin package comes with quite a lot of dependencies, so the downloading and installation might take some time.

Once the package starts installing, it will ask you whether or not you want to use Apache or lighttpd for phpMyAdmin's web server. Generally, unless you have a good reason to do otherwise, I'd recommend that you use Apache. (You can use the tab key to move the cursor while within the dialog box, if you get stuck.)

Next, the installer will ask if it can create and configure a database for phpMyAdmin using the dbconfig-common script. If you're a first-time user, and don't have advanced configuration needs, then use the tab key to select Yes and hit enter. The script will ask you for the password of your MySQL server's root user. Enter the password, and the installer will continue.

The installer will then ask for a password for phpMyAdmin's database user. Select a password for the database user. Remember, as always, to set a strong password, with a mixture of uppercase letters, lowercase letters, numerals, and punctuation. You'll then need to enter the password again.

After that, the installer will wrap up and return you to the command line. If you installed it locally, you can then access your new phpMyAdmin installation by opening up a web browser on your Ubuntu system and navigating to this address:

http://127.0.0.1/phpmyadmin

Enter your MySQL root user and password, and you'll have access to phpMyAdmin.

You can also access phpMyAdmin from a remote computer. For instance, if you installed phpMyAdmin on the machine with the IP address of 192.168.1.100, you would access it with this address:

http://192.168.1.100/phpmyadmin

13

INSTALLING WEB APPLICATIONS (WORDPRESS, MEDIAWIKI, AND MOODLE)

Hosting web applications is where Linux really shines. As we mentioned in Chapter II, Apache servers running on Linux or UNIX-like systems comprise around a third or so or so of the Internet. Ubuntu Linux can run a variety of web applications, ranging from simple interactive sites to powerful content management systems.

A "CONTENT MANAGEMENT SYSTEM" is a web application that lets people publish content to a website without deep knowledge of HTML or PHP coding. In this chapter, we'll discuss how to install three of the most popular content management systems on a Ubuntu web server – WordPress, MediaWiki, and Moodle. These three content management systems provide the backend for millions of websites across the Internet.

HOWEVER, WordPress, MediaWiki, and Moodle are all powered by something called a LAMP server, which we'll discuss in the next section.

The Lamp Server

LAMP is simply an acronym for Linux, Apache, MySQL, and PHP (or Perl and Python). These four software components provide a powerful web server and the backend of content management systems like WordPress, MediaWiki, and Moodle. In a LAMP server, Linux is the operating system. Apache is the web server, and MySQL the database backend.

WE'VE DISCUSSED both Apache and MySQL, but we haven't yet mentioned the "P" in "LAMP" - PHP. PHP is a "scripting language", which is a kind of computer language written specifically to control a particular software or hardware component. In this case, PHP was developed to control and manage dynamic web pages. (PHP originally stood for "Personal Home Page", but now stands for "PHP: Hypertext Processor.") WordPress, MediaWiki, and Moodle are all written to use PHP. In the next sections, we'll discuss how to install WordPress, MediaWiki, and Moodle on a Ubuntu machine.

(IF YOU READ straight through the next few sections, you'll notice that I'll repeat a lot of the directions we already discussed. There are two reasons for that. The first is that WordPress, MediaWiki, and Moodle all use a lot of the same software components. The second is that I wanted each web app to have its own complete set of instructions, so I don't have to say "next, install Apache like we discussed in Chapter 11", which means you don't have to scroll back and forth. I personally hate it when technical writers do that, so I'm not going to do that here. Besides, this is an ebook, so it's not as if repeating some directions will drive up the printing costs.)

Install Wordpress On Ubuntu

WordPress, first developed in 2003, is a content management system that runs quite a variety of websites. In WordPress's early days, it tended to run only personal blogs and smaller sites. However, the software improved considerably with every version, and it's adaptable enough to be used for a variety of different sites. WordPress's big break came in 2009 when popular blogging platform Movable Type made unpopular changes to its licensing terms. Enough Movable Type users were annoyed with the change to migrate to WordPress, and WordPress is the dominant open-source content management system on the Internet as of this writing.

It's QUITE possible to install WordPress on a machine running either the desktop or the server version of Ubuntu. This makes an excellent environment for testing and experimentation, since you can tweak and experiment to your heart's desire without rendering your production blog inoperable. If you need to run an internal corporate blog of some kind, hosting WordPress on an Ubuntu box or virtual machine is a cheaper solution than more expensive blogging or collaboration software. Or, if you're really ambitious (and you can afford the bandwidth), you can host an Internet-accessible WordPress blog out of your apartment.

LET's BEGIN!

(NOTE that the Ubuntu repositories now contain a fully automated WordPress installation. However, I believe that installing it by hand yourself has significant value – you'll not only learn how to set up a LAMP server, but installing step-by-step gives you valuable troubleshooting knowledge later on in case something breaks.)

.   .   .

FIRST, install Ubuntu into your machine of choice. Once Ubuntu is installed and updated, you will need to install five pieces of software: the Apache web server, the MySQL database server version 5.7, PHP version 7, the MySQL module for PHP, and finally the WordPress software itself.

FIRST, install the Apache web server. To install Apache, go to a Terminal window or a command prompt and type this command:

SUDO APT-GET INSTALL **apache2**

(TECHNICALLY, you'll be installing Apache 2, the latest version.)

ENTER YOUR PASSWORD TO AUTHENTICATE, follow the default prompts, and apt will download and install the Apache web server for you.

AND THAT'S IT! Apache should now be working. To test it from the web server itself, go to a web browser and visit the address http://127.0.0.1. You'll remember that this is the "local loopback" address, basically the address the computer uses to refer to itself. Alternatively, you could test it from another computer on the same subnet. For instance, if you installed Apache on a computer with an IP address of 192.168.1.100, you could test it by going to another computer on the same subnet and visiting http://192.168.100 from the web browser.

.   .   .

REGARDLESS, if Apache is working properly, you should see the default Apache/Ubuntu web page with the Ubuntu logo in the upper left-hand corner.

APACHE IS NOW OPERATIONAL.

THE NEXT STEP TO install WordPress is to install the MySQL database server. Return to the Terminal and type this command:

SUDO APT-GET **install mysql-server-5.7**

(As of this writing, MySQL Server version 5.7 is the latest version available in the Ubuntu repositories, though future versions of Ubuntu   may   receive   the   newer   versions   of MySQL.)

Enter your password to authenticate, and apt will download the MySQL files and install them for you. It's a big set of files, so depending on the speed of your Internet connection, it might take a while to download. After the files are downloaded and are installing, the installer will ask you for a password for MySQL's root user. Just as the root user in Linux has complete control over the system, the root user in MySQL has absolute control over all databases, tables, permissions, and users. For obvious security reasons, you'll want to create an extremely strong password (a mixture of uppercase, lower-case, numbers, and punctuation, the longer the better) for your MySQL root user.

(Note that in the password dialog box, if you can't get the <OK> field selected, you can use the tab key to jump from the text input line to the <OK> field.)

After you enter the root password, the installer will finish working with the MySQL files, and return you to the command line.

Next, you'll want to run the mysql_secure_installation script to tighten up security on your new MySQL server. Run this command from the prompt:

sudo mysql_secure_installation

First, the mysql_secure_installation script will ask you to enter the current password for the MySQL root user. After you do that, it will ask if you want to change the root password. Since you already set a root password, you can hit "n" (unless you want to change it again for some reason).

Next, the script will ask you to setup the VALIDATE PASSWORD plugin, which checks passwords for appropriate strength. Hit Y to accept, and then set the password strength level by hitting 0 for Low, 1, for Medium, and 2 for Strong.

Next, the script will ask if you want to remove the anonymous user. The anonymous user, like anonymous access in FTP, lets someone log into MySQL without having a proper user account. For security reasons, it's always best to remove the anonymous user, so hit "y" to continue.

After that, the script will ask if you want to prevent the MySQL root user from logging in remotely to the MySQL server. Always hit "y" to forbid root remote access, since if an attacker guesses your root password, he can destroy your databases or steal the information they contain.

After this, the script will ask if you want to remove the test database. MySQL includes a test database that anyone can access. Again, this is a security hole, so you'll want to hit "y" to remove the test database.

The script will then ask to reload the privilege tables so the changes take effect. Hit "y", and the   **mysql_secure_installation**   script will conclude and return you to the command line.

MySQL   server   is   now   installed   on   your   Ubuntu system.

THE NEXT STEP to installing WordPress is to install PHP version 7:

.   .   .

SUDO APT-GET install php

THEN INSTALL the MySQL module for PHP:

SUDO APT-GET install php-mysql

YOU MAY ALSO WANT to install the GD library for PHP, since many WordPress plugins rely on it for graphical manipulation (note that this is an optional step):

SUDO APT-GET install php-gd

FINALLY, download the WordPress software to your computer. You can obtain it from this address:

HTTP://WORDPRESS.ORG/LATEST.TAR.GZ

IF YOU'RE WORKING EXCLUSIVELY from the command line, you can use this command to download the WordPress software:

WGET HTTP://WORDPRESS.ORG/LATEST.TAR.GZ

USE this command to unpack the WordPress files:

.   .   .

tar -xzvf latest.tar.gz

MOVE the WordPress files over to the /var/www/html directory. (In this command, I'll assume you unpacked the WordPress files to your home directory; you will have to adjust the command if you unpacked them in a different directory.)

SUDO CP -R ~/WORDPRESS/* **/var/www/html/**

NOW THAT WE'VE got our software installed and downloaded, we'll need to configure it. First, we'll need to prepare MySQL for use with WordPress. WordPress requires a database and a database user, and full permission for its database user to access its database. To start the MySQL command-line client on Ubuntu 17.10 and earlier, use this command:

mysql -u root -p

ENTER the password for the MySQL root user, and you'll find yourself at the MySQL command prompt, which will look like this:

mysql>

IF YOU ARE USING MySQL on Ubuntu 18.04 and above, you will need to use the sudo command to launch the MySQL command line client:
   sudo mysql
   Enter your password, and if your account has administrative rights to your system, you will then enter the MySQL client.

Our next steps are to create a WordPress database, create a user to access that database, and grant our new user all rights to the Word-Press database.

(AN IMPORTANT NOTE before we continue, though. All commands made from the MySQL prompt must end with a semicolon to denote the end of the statement. Any commands that do not end with a semicolon will not work. With that in mind, let's first create a database.)

TO CREATE A DATABASE FOR WORDPRESS, use this command at the **mysql>** prompt:

CREATE DATABASE WORDPRESS;

THE MYSQL CLIENT will respond with a message that should say "Query OK, 1 row affect (0.00 sec)." This means the command was successful, and a new database named "newdatabase" has been created.

NEXT, you'll create a user who will access that database and assign a password to that user. In this example, we'll assign a password of "1234". However, in real life, just as with the root user, you'll want to assign a strong password. (This database user won't have full control over the MySQL user as the root user does, but we will give it full control over the database we just created, and a malicious user who guesses the password could cause all kinds of trouble.):

CREATE USER WORDPRESSUSER **IDENTIFIED BY** '1234';

. . .

YOU SHOULD GET THE "QUERY OK" message again. The final step is to assign all privileges on the "wordpress" database to the "wordpressuser" user. Use this command to assign the permissions:

GRANT ALL PRIVILEGES ON WORDPRESS.* **TO** WORDPRESSUSER **IDENTIFIED BY** '1234';

THAT ISN'T a typo - those are single quote marks (') instead of the usual double quote marks (") that were used in the command to set the password. MySQL's internal syntax, alas, isn't always consistent. Anyway, if you typed the command correctly, you should get the "Query OK" confirmation again.

ONCE YOU ARE DONE, use this command to quit the MySQL command-line interface:

exit

NOW THAT WE have MySQL prepared, we can now configure Word-Press itself. Specifically, we'll have to configure WordPress to talk to the database we just created. To do so, you must create a wp-config.php file in the WordPress directory. Fortunately, WordPress includes a handy wp-config-sample.php you can use as a template.

TYPE THIS COMMAND TO create a wp-config file (assuming you installed WordPress in the /var/www/html directory):

. . .

SUDO   CP   /var/www/html/wordpress/wp-config-sample.php
/var/www/html/wp-config.php

NEXT, use vi to edit the newly created wp-config file:

SUDO VI /var/www/html/wp-config.php

YOU'LL SEE that the wp-config.php file contains a number of variables. Change the following three variables:

-CHANGE PUTYOURDBNAMEHERE TO WORDPRESS .

-CHANGE USERNAMEHERE TO WORDPRESSUSER .

-CHANGE YOURPASSWORD HERE TO 1234 .

ONCE YOU HAVE your changes made (after double-checking the spelling, of course), switch vi to Command mode, and save your changed file.

ONCE IS THIS IS DONE, rename Apache's default index.html file to index.html.old. Otherwise Apache will access the default sample page instead of starting Wordpress:

sudo mv index.html index.html.old

. . .

EVERYTHING SHOULD NOW BE READY. Open up a web browser, and navigate to http://127.0.0.1/. (If you want to access it from a different machine, of course, use the IP address of the WordPress server, for instance – http://192.168.1.100.) If you configured everything correctly, you should then be greeted by the WordPress configuration page. You'll pick a username, and WordPress will assign you a password. Follow the prompts, and you will have a functional WordPress blog installed on a Ubuntu machine. Congratulations!

ONE FINAL NOTE: if you configure your blog from a local browser, it will probably set your blog's address as http://127.0.0.1. This is fine if you only want to view it from the host machine, but if you want to view it over the network, you'll need to change it. Fortunately, you can do so quickly by going Options in the WordPress admin interface, and then to General, and changing the blog's URL.

Installing Mediawiki On Ubuntu

Wikipedia, that encyclopedia of a thousand "citations needed", runs on an open-source web application called MediaWiki. A wiki, if you haven't heard the term before, is basically an online encyclopedia that relies on user contributions. Wikis can range from broad, general-topic encyclopedias like Wikipedia itself, or devoted to a single topic, like a television show or a computer game. You can quite easily install MediaWiki and host your own wiki off a Ubuntu system. Installing MediaWiki on Ubuntu takes three steps: first, you install the prerequisite software packages, second, you configure the prerequisites, and third, you install MediaWiki and run its configuration script.

LET'S BEGIN!

.   .   .

First, install Ubuntu into your machine of choice. Once Ubuntu is installed and updated, you will need to install five pieces of software: the Apache web server, the MySQL database server version 5.7, PHP version 7, the MySQL module for PHP, and finally the MediaWiki software itself.

First, install the Apache web server. To install Apache, go to a Terminal window or a command prompt and type this command:

SUDO APT-GET INSTALL **apache2**

(Technically, you'll be installing Apache 2, the latest version.)

Enter your password to authenticate, follow the default prompts, and apt will download and install the Apache web server for you.

And that's it! Apache should now be working. To test it from the web server itself, go to a web browser and visit the address http://127.0.0.1. You'll remember that this is the "local loopback" address, basically the address the computer uses to refer to itself. Alternatively, you could test it from another computer on the same subnet. For instance, if you installed Apache on a computer with an IP address of 192.168.1.100, you could test it by going to another computer on the same subnet and visiting http://192.168.100 from the web browser.

Regardless, if Apache is working properly, you should see the default Apache/Ubuntu web page with the Ubuntu logo in the upper left-hand corner.

Apache is now operational.

The next step to install MediaWiki is to install the MySQL database server. Return to the Terminal and type this command:

sudo apt-get install mysql-server-5.7

(As of this writing, MySQL Server version 5.7 is the latest version available in the Ubuntu repositories, though future versions of Ubuntu may receive the newer versions of MySQL.)

Enter your password to authenticate, and apt will download the MySQL files and install them for you. It's a big set of files, so depending on the speed of your Internet connection, it might take a while to download. After the files are downloaded and are installing, the installer will ask you for a password for MySQL's root user. Just as the root user in Linux has complete control over the system, the root user in MySQL has absolute control over all databases, tables, permissions, and users. For obvious security reasons, you'll want to create an extremely strong password (a mixture of uppercase, lowercase, numbers, and punctuation, the longer the better) for your MySQL root user.

(Note that in the password dialog box, if you can't get the <OK> field selected, you can use the tab key to jump from the text input line to the <OK> field.)

After you enter the root password, the installer will finish working with the MySQL files, and return you to the command line.

Next, you'll want to run the mysql_secure_installation script to tighten up security on your new MySQL server. Run this command from the prompt:

sudo mysql_secure_installation

First, the mysql_secure_installation script will ask you to enter the current password for the MySQL root user. After you do that, it will ask if you want to change the root password. Since you already set a root password, you can hit "n" (unless you want to change it again for some reason).

Next, the script will ask you to setup the VALIDATE PASSWORD plugin, which checks passwords for appropriate strength. Hit Y to accept, and then set the password strength level by hitting 0 for Low, 1, for Medium, and 2 for Strong.

Next, the script will ask if you want to remove the anonymous user. The anonymous user, like anonymous access in FTP, lets someone log into MySQL without having a proper user account. For security reasons, it's always best to remove the anonymous user, so hit "y" to continue.

After that, the script will ask if you want to prevent the MySQL root user from logging in remotely to the MySQL server. Always hit "y" to forbid root remote access, since if an attacker guesses your root password, he can destroy your databases or steal the information they contain.

After this, the script will ask if you want to remove the test database. MySQL includes a test database that anyone can access. Again, this is a security hole, so you'll want to hit "y" to remove the test database.

The script will then ask to reload the privilege tables so the changes take effect. Hit "y", and the **mysql_secure_installation** script will conclude and return you to the command line.

MySQL server is now installed on your Ubuntu system.

THE NEXT STEP to installing MediaWiki is to install PHP version 7:

SUDO APT-GET **install php**

. . .

THEN INSTALL the MySQL module for PHP:

SUDO APT-GET install php-mysql

THEN INSTALL the mbstring PHP module:

SUDO APT-GET install php-mbstring

THEN INSTALL the xml PHP module:

SUDO APT-GET install php-xml

NEXT, restart Apache with this command so that it reloads with all the PHP extensions enabled:

SUDO /etc/init.d/apache2 restart

FINALLY, download the MediaWiki software to your Desktop. You can obtain it from this address:

HTTPS://WWW.MEDIAWIKI.ORG/WIKI/DOWNLOAD

IF YOU'RE WORKING EXCLUSIVELY from the command line, you can use this command to download the MediaWiki software:

·   ·   ·

WGET HTTPS://RELEASES.WIKIMEDIA.ORG/MEDIAWIKI/1.30.0/MEDIAWIKI-1.30.0.TAR.GZ

(NOTE THAT THE VERSION NUMBER, and hence the file name, WILL change with future versions of MediaWiki, so double-check before downloading the file.)

USE this command to unpack the MediaWiki files:

tar -xzvf mediawiki-1.30.0.tar.gz

FINALLY, move the MediaWiki files over to the /var/www/html directory. (In this command, I'll assume you unpacked the MediaWiki files to your home directory; you will have to adjust the command if you unpacked them in a different directory.)

SUDO CP -R ~/MEDIAWIKI-1.30.0/* /var/www/html

NOW WE'LL NEED to prepare MySQL for use with MediaWiki. To start the MySQL command-line client on Ubuntu 17.10 and earlier, use this command:

mysql -u root -p

ENTER the password for the MySQL root user, and you'll find yourself at the MySQL command prompt, which will look like this:

. . .

mysql>

IF YOU ARE USING MySQL on Ubuntu 18.04 and above, you will need to use the sudo command to launch the MySQL command line client:

sudo mysql

Enter your password, and if your account has administrative rights to your system, you will then enter the MySQL client.

Our next steps are to create a MediaWiki database, create a user to access that database, and grant our new user all rights to the MediaWiki database.

(AN IMPORTANT NOTE before we continue, though. All commands made from the MySQL prompt must end with a semicolon to denote the end of the statement. Any commands that do not end with a semicolon will not work. With that in mind, let's first create a database.)

TO CREATE A DATABASE FOR MEDIAWIKI, use this command at the **mysql>** prompt:

CREATE DATABASE MEDIAWIKI;

THE MYSQL CLIENT will respond with a message that should say "Query OK, 1 row affect (0.00 sec)." This means the command was successful, and a new database named "newdatabase" has been created.

. . .

NEXT, you'll create a user who will access that database and assign a password to that user. In this example, we'll assign a password of "1234". However, in real life, just as with the root user, you'll want to assign a strong password. (This database user won't have full control over the MySQL user as the root user does, but we will give it full control over the database we just created, and a malicious user who guesses the password could cause all kinds of trouble.):

CREATE USER MEDIAWIKIUSER **IDENTIFIED BY** '1234';

AGAIN YOU SHOULD GET the "Query OK" confirmation message. The final step is to assign all privileges on the "mediawiki" database to the "mediawikiuser" user. Use this command to assign the permissions:

GRANT ALL PRIVILEGES ON MEDIAWIKI.* **TO** MEDIAWIKIUSER **IDENTIFIED BY** '1234';

THAT ISN'T a typo - those are single quote marks (') instead of the usual double quote marks (") that were used in the command to set the password. MySQL's internal syntax, alas, isn't always consistent. Anyway, if you typed the command correctly, you should get the "Query OK" confirmation again.

ONCE YOU ARE DONE, use this command to quit the MySQL command-line interface:

exit

. . .

ONCE IS THIS IS DONE, rename Apache's default index.html file to index.html.old. Otherwise Apache will access the default sample page instead of starting Wordpress:

sudo mv index.html index.html.old

ONCE THE PERMISSIONS have been set, launch the installation script by navigating here in your Ubuntu system's web browser:

HTTP://127.0.0.1

THE INSTALLATION SCRIPT is simply a web form you'll need to fill out. The default settings will work for the most part. You'll need to pick a name for your wiki, and you'll also need to enter the database name, the database user, and the password you created for MySQL. You will also need to set an administrator username and password for the wiki. Once you have appropriate information entered, complete the script, and MediaWiki will be installed.

HOWEVER, you'll need to do one more thing to finish the installation. After you complete the install script, MediaWiki will generate a LocalSettings.php file and offer it to you for download. Make sure to download the file and then transfer it to the /var/www/html file in order to complete the installation. (You may need to use SSH and SFTP to do this - see Chapter 10 on how to set them up.)

. . .

MEDIAWIKI SHOULD NOW BE FUNCTIONING on your Ubuntu system.

Installing Moodle On Ubuntu

Moodle is a virtual learning environment used by tens of thousands of schools across the world. Using Moodle, you can create a fully online course, or use it to supplment a traditionally-taught classroom course. Best of all, Moodle is free, and you can install it on Ubuntu. Installing Moodle on Ubuntu is a bit of work, but once it is finished, you'll have a robust e-learning server application.

It's quite possible to install Moodle on a machine running either the desktop or the server version of Ubuntu. This makes an excellent environment for testing and experimentation, since you can tweak and experiment to your heart's desire without rendering your production site inoperable. Given that Moodle is free, if you have a bit of Linux knowledge, you can use Moodle in lieu of far more expensive alternatives.

Let's begin!

First, install Ubuntu into your machine of choice. Once Ubuntu is installed and updated, you will need to install five pieces of software: the Apache web server, the MySQL database server version 5.7, PHP version 7, the MySQL module for PHP, and finally the WordPress software itself.

FIRST, install the Apache web server. To install Apache, go to a Terminal window or a command prompt and type this command:

SUDO APT-GET INSTALL **apache2**

(TECHNICALLY, you'll be installing Apache 2, the latest version.)

·   ·   ·

ENTER YOUR PASSWORD TO AUTHENTICATE, follow the default prompts, and apt will download and install the Apache web server for you.

AND THAT'S IT! Apache should now be working. To test it from the web server itself, go to a web browser and visit the address http://127.0.0.1. You'll remember that this is the "local loopback" address, basically the address the computer uses to refer to itself. Alternatively, you could test it from another computer on the same subnet. For instance, if you installed Apache on a computer with an IP address of 192.168.1.100, you could test it by going to another computer on the same subnet and visiting http://192.168.100 from the web browser.

REGARDLESS, if Apache is working properly, you should see the default Apache/Ubuntu web page with the Ubuntu logo in the upper left-hand corner.

APACHE IS NOW OPERATIONAL.

THE NEXT STEP TO install WordPress is to install the MySQL database server. Return to the Terminal and type this command:

sudo apt-get install mysql-server-5.7

(As of this writing, MySQL Server version 5.7 is the latest version available in the Ubuntu repositories, though future versions of Ubuntu may receive the newer versions of MySQL.)

Enter your password to authenticate, and apt will download the MySQL files and install them for you. It's a big set of files, so depending on the speed of your Internet connection, it might take a while to download. After the files are downloaded and are installing, the installer will ask you for a password for MySQL's root user. Just as the root user in Linux has complete control over the system, the root user in MySQL has absolute control over all databases, tables, permissions, and users. For obvious security reasons, you'll want to create an extremely strong password (a mixture of uppercase, lowercase, numbers, and punctuation, the longer the better) for your MySQL root user.

(Note that in the password dialog box, if you can't get the <OK> field selected, you can use the tab key to jump from the text input line to the <OK> field.)

After you enter the root password, the installer will finish working with the MySQL files, and return you to the command line.

Next, you'll want to run the mysql_secure_installation script to tighten up security on your new MySQL server. Run this command from the prompt:

sudo mysql_secure_installation

First, the mysql_secure_installation script will ask you to enter the current password for the MySQL root user. After you do that, it will ask if you want to change the root password. Since you already set a root password, you can hit "n" (unless you want to change it again for some reason).

Next, the script will ask you to setup the VALIDATE PASSWORD plugin, which checks passwords for appropriate strength. Hit Y to accept, and then set the password strength level by hitting 0 for Low, 1, for Medium, and 2 for Strong.

Next, the script will ask if you want to remove the anonymous user. The anonymous user, like anonymous access in FTP, lets someone log into MySQL without having a proper user account. For security reasons, it's always best to remove the anonymous user, so hit "y" to continue.

After that, the script will ask if you want to prevent the MySQL root user from logging in remotely to the MySQL server. Always hit "y" to forbid root remote access, since if an attacker guesses your root password, he can destroy your databases or steal the information they contain.

After this, the script will ask if you want to remove the test database. MySQL includes a test database that anyone can access. Again, this is a security hole, so you'll want to hit "y" to remove the test database.

The script will then ask to reload the privilege tables so the changes take effect. Hit "y", and the **mysql_secure_installation** script will conclude and return you to the command line.

MySQL server is now installed on your Ubuntu system.

Now we'll need to prepare MySQL for use with Moodle. To start the MySQL command-line client on Ubuntu 17.10 and earlier, use this command:

mysql -u root -p

ENTER the password for the MySQL root user, and you'll find yourself at the MySQL command prompt, which will look like this:

mysql>

IF YOU ARE USING MySQL on Ubuntu 18.04 and above, you will need to use the sudo command to launch the MySQL command line client:

sudo mysql

Enter your password, and if your account has administrative rights to your system, you will then enter the MySQL client.

Our next steps are to create a Moodle database, create a user to access that database, and grant our new user all rights to the Moodle database.

(An important note before we continue, though. All commands made from the MySQL prompt must end with a semicolon to denote the end of the statement. Any commands that do not end with a semicolon will not work. With that in mind, let's first create a database.)

To create a database for Moodle, use this command at the mysql> prompt:

CREATE DATABASE moodle;

The MySQL client will respond with a message that should say "Query OK, 1 row affect (0.00 sec)." This means the command was successful, and a new database named "newdatabase" has been created.

Next, you'll create a user who will access that database and assign a password to that user. In this example, we'll assign a password of "1234". However, in real life, just as with the root user, you'll want to assign a strong password. (This database user won't have full control over the MySQL user as the root user does, but we will give it full control over the database we just created, and a malicious user who guesses the password could cause all kinds of trouble.):

CREATE USER moodleuser IDENTIFIED BY '1234';

Again you should get the "Query OK" confirmation message. The final step is to assign all privileges on the "moodle" database to the "moodleuser" user. Use this command to assign the permissions:

GRANT ALL PRIVILEGES ON moodle.* TO moodleuser IDEN-TIFIED BY '1234';

That isn't a typo – those are single quote marks (') instead of the usual double quote marks (") that were used in the command to set the password. MySQL's internal syntax, alas, isn't always consistent. Anyway, if you typed the command correctly, you should get the "Query OK" confirmation again.

Once you are done, use this command to quit the MySQL command-line interface:

exit

The next step to installing Moodle is to install PHP version 5, along with the necessary PHP modules. First, install PHP 5 with this command:

sudo apt-get install php

After this, you will need to install several different PHP extensions not included with the default PHP 5 implementation on Ubuntu. First, install the MySQL module for PHP:

sudo apt-get install php-mysql

You must also install the GD library for PHP:

sudo apt-get install php-gd

The JSON extension is also required:

sudo apt-get install php-json

The CURL extension:

sudo apt-get install php-curl

The XML extension:

sudo-apt-get install php-xml

The XMLRPC extension:

sudo apt-get install php-xmlrpc

The ZIP extension:

sudo apt-get install php-zip

The MBSTRING extension:

sudo apt-get install php-mbstring

The SOAP extension:

sudo apt-get install php-soap

And, finally, the INTL extension:

sudo apt-get install php-intl

After all the plugins have installed, restart Apache so it recognizes the plugins properly:

sudo /etc/init.d/apache2 restart

Finally, download the Moodle software to your Desktop. You can obtain it from this address:

http://download.moodle.org

Move the Moodle files over to the /var/www/html directory. (In this command, I'll assume you unpacked the moodle files to your home directory; you will have to adjust the command if you unpacked them in a different directory.)

sudo cp -r ~/moodle/* /var/www/html

After that, rename the old index.html file in /var/www so Apache uses Moodle's PHP files for the site, not the index.html file:

sudo mv index.html index.html.old

Now that we've got our software downloaded, we'll need to configure it.

You will need to create a location for Moodle to save data files. Traditionally, the location is in /var/moodledata. (Creating the data directory inside the web server directory is an extremely bad idea, due to the resultant security holes.) To create the data directory, use this command:

sudo mkdir /var/moodledata

Use this command to change the owner of the directory to the Apache system user. In Ubuntu, the Apache system user is usually named www-data:

sudo chown www-data /var/moodledata

Then use this command to make the /var/moodledata directory writable to Moodle:

sudo chmod -R 744 /var/moodledata

Now that configuration and setup is complete, we are actually read to begin installing Moodle!

Fire up a web browser and navigate to the Moodle location to launch the web-based installer. If your server's IP address (for example) is 192.168.1.100, the address would look like this:

http://192.168.1.100

This will take you to the Moodle setup page.

First, select the language for your Moodle installation, and then click the Next button.

The installer will then ask for the locations of Moodle's directories. The defaults will work, especially if you already created the /var/moodledata directory as indicated above. Click the Next button to continue.

Moodle will then ask what kind of database server to use. Since we already set up our MySQL database, select "Improved MySQL" and then hit the Next button.

Then installer will then need you to input the information for the database and database user we created above. Since our MySQL server is on the same machine as Moodle, leave "localhost" for the Database Host field. Enter "moodle" for Database Name, "moodleuser" for Database User, and then '1234' for Database Password. Leave the other fields blank, and then click Next.

Moodle will then generate a config.php file. Copy and paste the data of the config.php file, save it as "config.php", and then transfer it to your server. Make sure to put it in the directory containing the Moodle installation – in this example, /var/www/html. Once the config.php is in place, make sure to mark it as executable with this command, otherwise the installation will halt:

sudo chmod 744 /var/www/html/config.php

Save config.php file, and then go back to the web browser and click the Next button.

Moodle will then ask if you agree to the terms of service. If you do, click the Continue button.

The installer will then run a system check to make sure your server has all the necessary software to support Moodle. If not (it's common to forget one of the PHP extensions), the installation will pause to allow you to install the missing software. Once you have, click Reload. If all the checks are passed, you can click the Continue button to continue.

The Moodle installer will then start building the database tables it requires in the database we created earlier. The Moodle database is large and complex, and building the database may take a considerable amount of time, so be patient. As the installer successfully builds database tables, they will scroll down in the browser window. Once the database construction is complete, the Continue button will appear at the very bottom of the page. Click on it to continue.

Moodle will then display a form for you to set up an administrator account for your new site. Enter an appropriate username and a strong password, along with any other required fields. Once you have finished, click on the Update Profile button at the bottom of the page.

The install will then ask you to pick a full site name and a short name for the site. Select suitable names, and then click the Save Changes button.

Congratulations! Your Moodle installation is now complete, and you can begin adding courses and other materials. For additional documentation, the Moodle site contains many useful resources:

http://docs.moodle.org/26/en/Main_page

14

THE EIGHT BEST APPLICATIONS FOR A NEW UBUNTU DESKTOP INSTALLATION

W e've been looking at how to set up Ubuntu as a server platform, but in this chapter we're going to shift gears and look at some of the best applications available for the Ubuntu desktop.

One of Ubuntu's big advantages over Microsoft Windows is the large number of applications included with a standard Ubuntu software install. With Microsoft Windows, you get a few games, a few utilities, and WordPad, which doesn't even include spell check. Ubuntu, on the other hand, comes with a wealth of preinstalled software. It includes LibreOffice, a full-featured free software suite. It comes with a variety of games, sound & video tools, utilities, productivity applications, and others. In fact, many users don't need to install additional software, simply because the applications included with Ubuntu are adequate to their needs.

However, there are a lot of excellent applications that are not included with the Ubuntu install disc. In this chapter, we're going to look at nine of the best applications for Ubuntu, and how to install them.

The Ubuntu Restricted Extras

The issue of media playback in Ubuntu is kind of a tricky one, legally speaking.

Every media file, whether video or audio, is encoded in digital form in a specific way. In order to decode the file so you can listen to it or watch it, it first needs to be decoded, using a specific piece of software called a "codec." This sounds simple enough, but codecs are often patented, which means they're legally protected, and one often has to pay licensing fees to use them.

The problem comes that most of the really popular media formats, like MP3 files, AAC files, and DVD, use codecs that are legally protected. Canonical and Ubuntu, following the lead of Debian, are committed to using free, legally unencumbered software whenever possible. So the codecs for MP3s, DVDs, AAC files, and numerous other media formats are not included by default in a new installation of Ubuntu.

Hence, the Ubuntu Restricted Extras package. This package includes the codecs for MP3, AAC, and other popular media formats, along with Microsoft's TrueType fonts. Installing the Ubuntu Restricted Extras package will allow you to use these media formats.

Note, however, that the Ubuntu Restricted Extras package may not be legal to use in your country. If it's not, then you shouldn't use it – for obvious reasons we're not going to advocate that anyone break the law.

(The default installer for Ubuntu will offer you the option of installing these items during the installation wizard.)

But if it is legal, installing the Ubuntu Restricted Extras package is quite easy. Simply launch Terminal by clicking on the Dash and searching for it in the search field. When the Terminal window opens up, type this command:

sudo apt-get install ubuntu-restricted-extras

Enter your password to authenticate, and apt will download and install the Restricted Extras package for you. The combined files are a couple hundred megabytes, so it might take some time depending on your connection speed. After the installation is done, you can then play most media formats on your Ubuntu system.

Vlc Media Player

VLC Media Player is a handy program that can play numerous forms of video, and runs on just about any OS platform. It also runs on Ubuntu, and installing it is quite simple.

First, open up a Terminal window and type this command:

sudo apt-get install vlc

Enter your password to authenticate, and apt will download and install VLC and its various dependencies for you. (You can also install it through Synaptic Package Manager and Ubuntu Software Center.) Afterwards you can launch VLC by clicking on the Application View button at the bottom of the Dock, searching for "VLC", and clicking on the VLC icon.

Of course, VLC needs codecs into order to display certain kinds of video. You may need to install the Ubuntu Restricted Extras package in order to get maximum use out of VLC.

Virtualbox Ose

Virtualization is an extremely useful software concept. If you're unfamiliar with the term, a "virtual machine" is a software process on a computer that mimics a separate, running computer. So, let's say you have a computer with Ubuntu and install some sort of virtualization software on it. You can then create virtual machines – one running say, Windows XP, another running Windows 7, and perhaps still another running Fedora Linux.

I have found virtualization to be incredibly useful in my work. In the old days, if you wanted to test an application or program, you had to install it on your primary machine, to dig up an old machine to test it – and that meant another monitor and keyboard and all the other attendant clutter on your desk. With virtualization, you can have a second OS running as a window your main machine.

There are a number of virtualization products available for Ubuntu, but in my opinion, Virtualbox OSE offers the best balance between ease of use and features. To install Virtualbox, simply go to a Terminal window and type this command:

sudo apt-get install virtualbox

And that's it! The apt utility will download Virtualbox and its dependencies, and then will then automatically execute its rather lengthy installation script. As ease of installation goes, you can't beat that. After the installation is finished, you can start Virtualbox by going to the Activities Overview, searching for "virtualbox", and clicking on the Virtualbox OSE icon.

Covering virtualization in depth is way beyond the scope of this book – entire books can (and have) been written about virtualization. But I urge you to experiment with it, as it is a superb and low-cost way of teaching yourself additional skills.

Google Chrome

The desktop edition of Ubuntu comes with the excellent Mozilla Firefox browser. However, Google's Chrome browser, released in late 2008, has gained a powerful following. Google makes Chrome available for a variety of platforms, and Ubuntu is no exception.

To install Chrome on Ubuntu, first visit the Google Chrome website:

http://www.google.com/chrome

Click on the Download button, which will take you to the download page. Select the 64-bit version for Ubuntu. Hit the accept and install button, and the Chrome installer will download.

Once the download is complete, you'll have a *.deb installer package for Chrome in your Downloads folder. Double-click on it to launch the installer. You'll be taken to the Ubuntu Software application. Click on the Install button to begin the installation of Chrome.

You'll need to enter your password to authenticate, and then follow the default prompts to install Chrome.

After the installation is complete, you can launch Chrome by clicking on the Application View button at the bottom of the Dock, searching for Chrome, and clicking on the Chrome icon.

Audacity

Another application Ubuntu lacks is an editor for digital audio. Which admittedly makes sense, as not that many people need to edit digital audio on a regular basis. If you do need to edit audio files, however, the Audacity application is excellent. And it's also available for Ubuntu.

To install Audacity, make your way to the Terminal window and type this command:

sudo apt-get install audacity

This will download and install Audacity and its dependencies from the Ubuntu repositories. Once finished, you can run Audacity by going to the Activities Overview, searching for "audacity", and clicking on the Audacity icon.

However, the default install of Audacity lacks the ability to export its projects as an MP3 file. To gain that functionality, you'll need to install the LAME library, which gives Audacity the ability to encode MP3 files. Note that the ownership of the MP3 patents remain in some dispute, so there may be liability issues in using LAME. However, if you're in the legal clear, you can use this Terminal command to install the LAME library:

sudo apt-get install libmp3lame0

This will gave Audacity the ability to export projects as MP3 files.

The Gimp

Starting with Ubuntu 10.04 Lucid Lynx, Ubuntu no longer came with the GNU Image Manipulation Tool (the GIMP), and all subsequent versions of Ubuntu follow in their predecessor's footsteps. This makes some sense; the GIMP is rather more image editing capability than your average user needs. However, some users want the GIMP back - it is a powerful and useful tool, and unlike Adobe Photoshop, it's free. (I prepare many of my ebook covers using the GIMP.) Fortunately, the packages are readily available in the Ubuntu repositories, and it's quite easy to install the GIMP. It only takes one Terminal command:

SUDO APT-GET **install gimp**

Enter your password to authenticate when prompted, and apt-get will download and install the GIMP for you. When the installation is complete, you can launch the GIMP by going to the Activities Overview, searching for "GIMP", and clicking on the application's icon.

Also, by default GIMP opens in three separate windows - one for the canvas itself, one for the toolbox, and one for dockable dialogs. If you want GIMP to run in single-window mode, with all three windows combined into one, go to the Windows menu and select Single-Window Mode.

Dropbox

Dropbox is a useful file-sharing and syncing service that lets you sync files between different machines over the Internet for free. It's very useful for backing up your important documents, pictures, MP3 files, video files, and other data. A Dropbox client that integrates with the Nautilus file manager is available for Ubuntu, and it's quite simple to install. Here's how to do it.

First, launch a new Terminal window by searching for Terminal in the Activities Overview, or by hitting the CTRL+ALT+T keys simultaneously. Once the Terminal launches, type this command at the prompt:

sudo apt-get install nautilus-dropbox

Enter this command, and then enter your password to authenticate. The apt-get utility will then download and install the Dropbox client for you.

Once the installation is complete, go to the Activities Overview again, search for "Dropbox", and click on the Dropbox icon. The

Dropbox application will launch, and will ask you to download Dropbox's proprietary Linux daemon. You will need to download the daemon to use Dropbox, so go ahead and allow the installation.

Once it is finished, Dropbox will launch. Enter your Dropbox credentials, and you can start using Dropbox with Ubuntu.

Filezilla

Ubuntu comes with both built-in command line SFTP and FTP clients, but if you find yourself working with file uploads a great deal, you might prefer to switch to a graphical FTP client for ease of use. Fortunately, the popular FileZilla FTP client is available for Ubuntu, and it's easy to install.

First, launch a new Terminal window by searching for Terminal in the Dash, or by hitting the CTRL+ALT+T keys simultaneously. Once the Terminal launches, type this command at the prompt:

sudo apt-get install filezilla

Enter this command, and then enter your password to authenticate. The apt-get utility will then download and install the FileZilla FTP client for you.

Once the installation is complete, go to the Activities Overview again, search for "FileZilla", and click on the FileZilla icon. Once the application launches, you can create a new connection by going to the File menu, selecting Site Manager, and entering the information for the site to which you wish to connect.

15

CREATE A BOOTABLE USB FLASH DRIVE

W hen you installed Ubuntu on your computer, odds are that you used a burned CD-ROM to do it.

But, let's face it – CD-ROMs are a pain to use. Compared to hard drives or USB flash drives, they're quite slow, since even the fastest optical drive can't keep up with a hard drive or a flash drive. They're also quite noisy, and it can become annoying to listen to the optical drive endlessly grinding away.

And depending on the age of the computer, there's an excellent chance the optical drive might just break down. As we discussed in the Introduction, one of Ubuntu's strengths (and the strengths of its low-footprint variants, like Xubuntu) is that it has lower system requirements than most versions of Windows, so it can be installed on older computers that might not have the horsepower to run the latest version of Windows. Optical drives have motors, and motors break down. Several times I've attempted to install Ubuntu or Xubuntu on an older machine, only to have the optical drive break down from the strain of attempting to boot off a CD.

This is where a bootable USB flash drive comes into the picture. Ubuntu includes a utility that lets you turn a USB flash drive into a bootable USB disk. Using this modified flash drive, you can bypass the CD-ROM drive entirely and boot a computer into Ubuntu using the flash drive (assuming the computer's BIOS supports booting from the USB ports, of course). Flash memory has no moving parts, so it's less likely to break down, and it's also faster and quieter than a CD-based installation. These flash drives are also useful for troubleshooting purposes – if you have a Windows system that won't boot, for instance, you can boot it up from a Ubuntu USB flash drive, and copy any critical documents to an external hard drive. (I personally have done this hundreds of times for clients in possession of a Windows machine that would no longer boot.)

In the next section, we'll show you how to create a bootable Ubuntu USB flash drive using the Startup Disk Creator utility.

Creating A Bootable Usb Flash Drive

To create the bootable USB flash drive, you'll need two things. The first is a USB flash drive, obviously, and it needs to be one gigabyte or larger in size. The second is an ISO image of a desktop Ubuntu disc. You can get the latest version of the desktop Ubuntu installation disc at this web address:

https://www.ubuntu.com/download

Once you've got both the ISO and the flash drive, you can begin. First, connect your flash drive to your Ubuntu computer. Then click on the Dash and search for "Startup Disk Creator" in the search field.

When the utility starts, it will ask for a Ubuntu installation disc. This is where the ISO file comes into play. Navigate the utility to your ISO file, adjust the slider to indicate how much reserved space for the Ubuntu files you want on the flash drive, and then click the Make Startup Disk button.

You'll then see a progress bar as the utility copies the Ubuntu files to your flash drive.

Note that this process may take several minutes.

Once it's done you'll see a message informing you that the installation is complete.

You can now use your flash drive to boot a computer into Ubuntu.

16

GAMING

S o far in this book we've talked a lot about the command line, server applications, and desktop productivity applications, but you can also have fun with your computer. (Though installing Samba, of course, is its own special kind of fun!) There is a wealth of computer game software available for Ubuntu, and in this chapter I'll discuss some of my favorites.

However, we must first make an uncomfortable admission. The gaming experience on Ubuntu is generally not as good as the gaming experience on a Microsoft Windows machine, a mobile device like an iPad or iPhone or a Kindle Fire, and a dedicated game console like an XBox or a Playstation. This is because while Linux dominates in the server room, it retains only a tiny desktop usage share, and consequently major game publishers tend to release their games only for Windows machines, mobile devices, and game consoles. (In fact, it tends to cause something of a stir when a game publisher releases a title for both Windows *and* Mac OS X.) It is possible to get major Windows games to play on Ubuntu using Wine, but it's a lot of work and not always reliable (we'll discuss that more in the next chapter).

That said, in the six years since the first edition of this book was published, the situation has changed quite a bit. The biggest platform for gaming, Steam, now works on Ubuntu Linux, and many games have been made available for Ubuntu. Another popular game store, GOG.com, offers many classic DOS games for Ubuntu via the DOSBox utility, and even a few newer games like Pillars Of Eternity or FTL: Faster Than Light.

Because of the changes over the last few years, there are quite a few enjoyable native games for Ubuntu. We'll discuss a few of the classic ones here. And while playing modern Windows games on a Ubuntu system is a challenge, playing old DOS game is a breeze, ironically enough – we'll show you how to do that as well.

Chess

Mac OS X and some editions of Windows 7 used to come with a chess game, but Ubuntu does not. Ubuntu does come with the usual assortment of free games – Solitaire, a tile game, some word puzzles – but no chess games. Fortunately, restoring Ubuntu to chess parity with Mac OS X and Windows 7 is quite easy. There is a package of free software called GNOME Games, and it includes a chess game. And as the GNOME Games package is native to Linux, it's quite easy to install on Ubuntu.

Simply go to the Terminal and type this command:

sudo apt-get install gnome-games

Enter your password to authenticate, and apt will download and install the missing GNOME Games. After the installation is complete, you can find Chess by clicking on the Activities Overview and searching for "Chess." You also get close to a dozen other free games with the GNOME Games pack; my favorite is Quadrapassel, a clone of the venerable Tetris puzzle game.

The Battle For Wesnoth

In turn-based strategy games, you assemble resources, build armies, and lead your troops in battle against your opponents. In fantasy-turn based games, you do all that, but you can also use magical fireballs and lightning bolts to smite your opponents, and also raise magical creatures like dragons and elves to fill the ranks of your armies.

"The Battle For Wesnoth" is a free turn-based strategy game available for Windows, Mac, and almost all Linux platforms. A volunteer-supported project, the game has been around since 2003. I've played it from time to time since 2006 or so, and "Wesnoth" has improved immensely in that time. The current incarnation of "The Battle For Wesnoth" is smooth, polished, and quite enjoyable to play.

And best of all, "Wesnoth" is both free and simple to install on Ubuntu. To install "Wesnoth", simply go to a Terminal prompt and type this command:

sudo apt-get install wesnoth

Put in your password to authenticate, and apt will download and install Wesnoth. The combined files are about 500 megabytes in size, so it might take some time. After the installation is complete, you can launch "Battle" by going to the Dash, searching for "Wesnoth", and clicking on the Battle for Wesnoth icon.

Angband

Those of you who have been playing computer games long enough might remember the old Rogue style computer games. The Rogue games originated in 1980 with the original Rogue game, written to be played on university UNIX computer terminals. In Rogue, the player took the role of an adventurer descending ever deeper into an elaborate dungeon, slaying monsters, avoiding traps, and collecting gold and experience. (This, of course, remains a staple of computer gaming to this day.) The "Roguelike" games descended from the original Rogue game, improving on its ideas and execution, and many graphical games run off the original principles of Rogue to this day.

Angband is one of the more prominent Roguelike games. Started in 1990, the game has been developed ever since then, and remains a classic Roguelike gaming experience, though with modern improvements to smooth over some of Rogue's original rough edges.

Installing Angband is pretty simple. Go to a Terminal window and use this command:

sudo apt-get install angband

Follow the default prompts and Angband will be installed. Once Angband is installed, you can start the game with this command:

angband

Follow the prompts to create your character and soon you'll soon be playing. Watch out for the goblins!

Dosbox

It is indeed a remarkable irony that it's often no longer possible to play old DOS games on Windows 10, but with proper software, you can play the same old games on Ubuntu. All you need is DOSBox, an emulation environment that lets you run old DOS games. As an added bonus, DOSBox is quite easy to install. Simply go to a Terminal window and type this command:

sudo apt-get install dosbox

Follow the default prompts, and DOSBox will install itself and a few other necessary packages on your Ubuntu system. After DOSBox is installed, you can launch it by going the Dash and searching for "DOSBox" in the search field. Or you can launch it from the command line:

dosbox

Now, since DOSBox relies on the old DOS system of drive letters, and Ubuntu Linux does not, you may be wondering how to mount your drives. Fortunately, this is quite simple. Let's say you create a directory named dos in your home directory to serve as the C: drive during your DOS session. To mount as a C: drive, use this command while in DOSBox:

mount c ~/dos

To mount your optical drive as a D: drive, use this command:

mount d -t cdrom /media/cdrom

Using these commands, you should be able to play a good many old DOS games on your Ubuntu system.

Steam

Valve made its popular Steam platform available for Ubuntu. Using the Steam client, you can play a number of popular games quite easily on your Ubuntu system (assuming your computer's hardware meets the system requirements for the various games). Installing the Steam client on Ubuntu is an easy and streamlined process, and we'll show you how to do it.

First, visit the Steam site and download the client:

http://store.steampowered.com

Click on the Install Steam button at the top of the page, and then the Install Steam Now button. This will download a .deb installer file to your Downloads folder. After the download has completed, navigate to your Downloads folder, and double-click on the installer to launch it.

After a moment the install will take you to the Ubuntu Software application and show you some information about Steam. Click on the Install button, and the Ubuntu Software application will ask for your password. Enter your password, and Ubuntu Software will install the client.

After the installation is complete, you can launch the Steam client by going to the Dash and searching for "Steam". When the client launches for the first time, it will likely downloaded several hundred megabytes worth of updates.

Once the download is finished, you can log into the client and peruse your library of Steam games.

Gog.Com

One of the best developments for Linux gaming in the past ten years has been the rise of GOG.com. The site began as Good Old Games in 2008, devoted to acquiring the rights to legally sell "abandonware" games, old DOS games that had been abandoned by their publishers for whatever reason.

GOG.com 2008, originally Good Old Games, improved to GOG.com in 2010. GOG.com currently offers numerous older DOS games now repackaged to run smoothly on Ubuntu. In this example, we will show you how to install Darklands, a classic Microprose RPG from 1992. The installation for Darklands is pretty typical, and you can use this example to install other older GOG.com games on Ubuntu.

First, log into your GOG.com account and download the Ubuntu installer for the game you wish to play. The installer will download as a shell script, which you will need to first mark as executable. To mark the shell script for Darklands as executable, launch the Terminal by hitting the CTRL+ATL+T keys simultaneously, and then enter this command

chmod +x ~/Downloads/gog_darklands_2.0.0.7.sh

Then execute the shell script with this command:

~/Downloads/gog_darklands_2.0.0.7.sh

This will launch the GOG.com installer for Darklands. Accept the EULA, and then select the destination folder for the installation. The default destinations are usually acceptable, unless you have a specific reason for installing the game elsewhere. The installer will then ask if you want to create a desktop shortcut and a menu item (this will allow you to find the game to launch it through the Dash). Make sure to select both, as it will make it easier to launch the game after the installer has finished.

Once the installation as finished, you can launch the game by going to the Dash, searching for "Darklands", and then double-clicking on the icon for Darklands. Ubuntu will then launch DOSBox and load Darklands preconfigured for you.

Note that the game will load full-screen – you can switch to the windowed mode by hitting the ALT and the ENTER keys simulta-neously.

This procedure will let you install most of GOG.com's Ubuntu-compatible classic games.

GOG.com also has a number of newer games that run natively on Ubuntu, though they only tend to be supported on older LTS versions of Ubuntu. Be sure to check the system requirements, since they will display a list of any software packages you might need to run the game. You can usually install these packages from the Terminal with the **apt-get** command.

17

RUN WINDOWS SOFTWARE WITH WINE

I 've helped many people try Ubuntu after switching from Windows, and they all inevitably have the same question.

"Hey, Ubuntu is great! But how can I install my favorite Windows application on it?"

On the surface, it seems like the obvious answer would be no. Windows software is written for the Windows platform, and Ubuntu software is written for the Linux platform, and never the two shall meet. If you want to use your favorite Windows application with Ubuntu, you need to either find a Linux version, or find another application that performs the task you want to do.

However, there's a way around that.

That way is a software application called "Wine", an acronym that means "Wine Is Not An Emulator." It's actually a compatibility layer that lets you, in theory, run Windows applications on a Linux system. Not all applications work, some work better than others, and some require considerable tweaking before they will work. However, if you're willing to do the research, you can get your Windows application working on Ubuntu.

In the next section, we'll look at installing and configuring Wine on an Ubuntu system. We'll also talk a bit about using Ubuntu to connect to Windows Server Terminal Services / Remote Desktop Services systems.

Installing And Configuring Wine

Configuring Wine can occasionally be a challenge, but Wine installs quite easily and runs just fine on Ubuntu. To install Wine, use this command at the Terminal prompt:

sudo apt-get install wine-stable

Enter your password to authenticate, and apt will download and install Wine. The combined packages come to a little over a hundred megabytes, so it might take a while to install depending upon your connection speed.

After the installation is finished, you can use the command line Wine program to install Windows software.

However, you'll probably first need to mark the installer file as executable. Depending on the application, Wine might not be able to install it if its installer file isn't executable. (We discussed file permissions in Chapter 2.) For instance, to mark an installer file in your Downloads folder named INSTALL.EXE as executable, use this command at the Terminal prompt:

chmod 755 ~/Downloads/INSTALL.EXE

After the file has been marked as executable, you can then install Windows software with Wine through the command line. For instance, to install the example above, you would use this command:

wine ~/Downloads/INSTALL.EXE

If the application did not install, you'll probably have to change the Wine settings. The best course is to probably browse the Wine application database and see if you can find the correct settings there. The database contains settings and tips for installing thousands of Windows applications, and you can find it here:

http://appdb.winehq.org/

Generally, Wine is very good at backwards compatibility - the older an application is, the more likely it is that Wine will support it.

Finally, you can install a Windows application through a

companion GUI application called Winetricks. Winetricks makes installing an application smooth and easy - but only if the specific application is supported. To install Winetricks, use this command at the Terminal:

sudo apt-get install winetricks

Once Winetricks is installed, you can launch it by going to the Dash, searching for "winetricks", and clicking on the icon for the application. Winetricks offers a GUI for installing Windows applications, and you can easily follow the prompts to install a supported Windows application.

Install Remmina

Microsoft Windows Servers have a technology called Terminal Services, renamed to Remote Desktop Services in Windows Server 2008 R2. This allows client computers to remotely connect to the server, viewing the remote desktop and using the remote applications as if they were installed locally. Many organization use Terminal Services/ Remote Desktop Services to centralize their computing infrastructures. That way an organization can have a powerful central server system, and use cheaper client computers to connect to the Terminal Services / Remote Desktop Services server.

Every version of Windows since Windows XP comes with an included Remote Desktop client. However, Remote Desktop provides an opportunity for you to use Ubuntu in a Windows-heavy environment. Versions of Ubuntu prior to 11.04 Natty Narwhal used a program called TSclient as a Remote Desktop client. It worked, but not very well.

However, there's a far superior option available now – Remmina. Ubuntu 11.04 Natty Narwhal (and all later versions of Ubuntu) includes Remmina as the default Remote Desktop client. Remmina has many more advanced features, and the biggest one is that it works much better on a netbook screen, and gives you greater options for selection the resolution. It also includes scroll bars for a Terminal Services window larger than the current screen size – an invaluable feature that TSClient just didn't have. If you have an older version of Ubuntu, you can install Remmina with this command at the Terminal windows:

sudo apt-get install remmina

Enter your password to authenticate, and apt-get will download and install Remmina for you. After the installation is complete, you can launch Remmina by going to the Applications menu, to Internet, and clicking on the Remmina icon. In Ubuntu 11.04 Natty Narwhal, you can also launch Remmina by clicking on the Dash and searching for it in the search field.

18

MANAGING AND CREATING EBOOKS ON UBUNTU

T his book only exists in ebook format, so if you're reading it, you're already familiar with ebooks as a concept. However, in the last few years (2007 to 2016, as of this writing), ebooks have taken the world by storm. Major online retailers report higher sales of ebooks than physical books, the sales of printed books and newspapers are collapsing, and bookstores are going out of business right and left. In my opinion, ebooks are as big a revolution as Gutenberg's printing press or the invention of paper. And like the printing press, I think ebooks will result in a widespread increase in literacy, as an entire generation of men and women who have never purchased a physical book will nonetheless read on their computer screens or smartphones.

Fortunately, you can use Ubuntu to both manage and create ebooks, using a variety of free software tools that we will discuss in this chapter.

What Is An Ebook?

An ebook, generally, is a book-length document stored in a digital file. Ebooks have been around almost since the beginning of the Internet – Project Gutenberg, which hosts an enormous number of free public domain ebooks, was founded in 1971. Publishers have been experimenting with digital formats, mostly unsuccessfully, ever since the World Wide Web became popular in the late 1990s. However, the lack of a viable ereaders hampered early adoption of ebooks. Only a very few people enjoyed reading a full-length book on a CRT monitor or on the tiny screen of a PDA device.

This changed with the development of e-Ink and LED tablet devices towards the end of the first decade of the 21st century. A quality e-Ink reading device provides an experience almost as good as a printed page, and a decent LED display, while not as good as an e-Ink device for sustained reading, nonetheless is much easier to read than an old tube monitor. With the increasing ubiquity of Internet connections, and the decreasing cost of ereader devices, the ebook revolution is well underway.

Paper books will never go away – radio was superseded by first television and then the Internet, but there are no shortages of commercial radio stations – but ebooks offer a number of useful advantages over paper books. The first is portability – four gigabytes of flash memory can hold thousands of ebooks. The equivalent amount of paper books would fill several rooms. The second is a positive environmental impact – ebooks are far easier on the environment (and the forests, specifically) than paper books, and due to the antiquated returns system employed by most modern publishers and bookstores, thousands of paper books are wasted every year. The third advantage is cost – ebooks are often cheaper than their physical counterparts, and vast numbers of public domain books, including the classics of Western civilization, are available for free from Project Gutenberg and other sites.

Ebook Formats

Ebooks come in a variety of formats, but there are two dominant ones – the MOBI format, and the EPUB format.

The MOBI format originated with a company called Mobipocket, which developed the MOBI format for ebooks and several different applications for reading MOBI files. Online retailer Amazon bought Mobipocket in 2005, and when the Kindle debuted in 2007, Amazon used the MOBI format for its Kindle books. Any ebook purchased off Amazon's site will be in the MOBI format.

EPUB is the second dominant ebook format. Established in 2007, it evolved out of the old Open eBook standard. EPUB is an open standard, which means that anyone can use it without paying license fees. It is comparatively easy to work with, too, since it relies upon CSS and XHTML for the book layout. Barnes & Noble uses EPUB for their online store, along with Kobo, Google Play, and most of the other major ebook vendors.

(To generalize, Amazon uses MOBI, while pretty much everyone else uses EPUB.)

Because of this, there's an annoying two-way split in the world of ebooks, much like the old fight over Betamax and VHS in the dawn of the VCR era. Many devices only read MOBI and not EPUB and vice-versa. Fortunately, a number of free tools exist to convert one format to another, which we shall discuss in the next section.

Convert And Manage Ebooks With Calibre

Because ebooks are often much cheaper than physical books, it is easy to quickly accumulate a large collection. Managing and organizing an ebook library can become something of a challenge. To make matters more complicated, the format war we discussed in the previous section means that some ebooks will work with one device, and others will not, and very few will work on both.

Fortunately, a free application called Calibre can solve a number of these problems. Originally developed in 2006, Calibre is an ebook management program. It automatically sorts your ebooks by title and author, which makes locating any single title much easier. It also can convert most ebook formats, allowing you to smoothly move from EPUB to MOBI and back again (so long as the files are not encrypted

– Calibre cannot read ebook files protected by digital rights management technologies – DRM). Calibre also contains a built-in ebook reader that can handle most ebook formats.

Calibre is also very easy to install, and you can install it through the Ubuntu Software application. (We discussed how to use the Ubuntu Software application to install software in Chapter 4.) It is, of course, quicker and easier to install Calibre using this terminal command:

sudo apt-get install calibre

Enter your password to authenticate, follow the default prompts, and apt will install Calibre for you.

After the installation is complete, you can launch Calibre via searching for it through the Activities Overview. The first time Calibre runs, you'll see a wizard asking for some configuration options: where to store your Calibre library, what eBook reader you use (if any), and what settings that eBook reader uses. Enter the appropriate information, and you can start using Calibre.

Calibre's GUI is reasonably easy to use, and the program includes a complete manual (in ebook form, of course).

Create Ebooks With Sigil

Reading ebooks is simple enough, but suppose you want to create an ebook? Where do you start?

The free Sigil application is a WYSIWYG ("what you see is what you get") editor that allows you to create EPUB files. Sigil is, as an application, fairly bare-bones, but with a bit of practice, you can create elaborate EPUB books with relative ease. (The EPUB version of this book was created with Sigil.) Sigil also lets you view the underlying XHTML code of an EPUB book, allowing you to make advanced changes to your book. Even better, it only takes a few terminal command to install Sigil on Ubuntu.

Here's how to do it.

First, launch the Terminal by hitting the CTRL+ALT+T keys simultaneously, and then enter this command:

sudo apt-get install sigil

Enter your password to authenticate, and Ubuntu will download and install Sigil for you.

ONCE THE INSTALLATION IS COMPLETE, you can launch Sigil by going to the Activities Overview, searching for "Sigil", and clicking on its icon.

19

CONVERTING AUDIO AND VIDEO

lmost all modern computers are "multimedia" computers – that is, they can play sound and video. This was not always the case – early personal computers relied entirely upon text-based interfaces, and only gradually added support for images, sounds, and video playback. In Ubuntu Linux, the text-based interface has not gone away (most of this book has discussed using the command line, after all), but a Ubuntu system is just as capable with multimedia as any Windows box or Macintosh laptop.

In this chapter we'll discuss how to convert different multimedia formats, but first we'll take a look at those multimedia formats themselves.

What Is A File Format?

When we talk about a multimedia file format, or a "codec", we refer to a way of storing audio and video data in digital form. A sound or video is an analog form of data (basically, a long wave). Computers, however, store data in digital format – in long strings of ones and zeroes. A "codec", therefore, is a piece of software that converts those ones and zeroes into an analog wave that you can play over your computer speakers.

As you might expect, there are many different standards for converting the ones and zeroes to analog waves and back again, and we'll look at a few of those competing standards in the next section.

Audio File Formats

There are several competing formats for music and audio files. However, one of them is clearly dominant – the MP3 format. Developed in 1993 by the Moving Pictures Expert Group, MP3 is the most common format for digital music files. Almost all the major online retailers sell music files in MP3 format, and almost all operating systems either play MP3 files by default or can easily acquire the capacity to play them.

Despite its ubiquity, MP3 is encumbered with a number of legal problems. Due a complicated series of lawsuits, no one is entirely certain who owns some of the patents connected with MP3, so anyone wanting to use the MP3 codec with their software or hardware needs to pay a licensing fee. Because of this, MP3 support is not included by default in Ubuntu – you need to explicitly enabled it during the installation process, or later by installing the Ubuntu Restricted Extras package (we'll discuss that later this chapter).

Though MP3 is the major digital audio format, there are several other significant ones as well. Windows Media Audio, WMA, is the default media format for Microsoft Windows, and in the late 90s and early 2000s, Microsoft hoped it would replace MP3. However, the Apple iPod came to dominate the digital music market during the 2000s, and Apple obviously had no interest in using one of Microsoft's formats. These days, WMA tends to only play on Windows machines and devices, and little else. Like MP3, WMA does not play by default on Ubuntu without the Restricted Extra package due to patent issues.

AAC, Advanced Audio Coding, is another major audio format, as it is the default audio format for Apple's iTunes software. AAC is designed to be the eventual replacement for the MP3 standard, and can compress more information into a smaller space than MP3. Again, however, due to patent issues, AAC support is not included in Ubuntu without the Restricted Extras package.

A final major audio format is OGG/Vorbis. Unlike the other major formats mentioned here, OGG/Vorbis is free and open source, which means that companies can use it without paying licensing fees. Therefore Ubuntu supports it without any additional packages. However, OGG/Vorbis remains in the minority, and only a very small amount of digital media is available in the format.

Video File Formats

Unlike audio file formats, there is not yet a single dominant video file format, but instead several major competing ones.

The oldest of the common video formats is Audio Video Interleave, or AVI. Introduced by Microsoft in the 1990s, AVI is comparatively primitive. Its biggest flaw is that it supports no compression whatsoever, which means that AVI files can become absolutely enormous. However, AVI works with numerous different applications and devices, so it remains in use.

WMV, Windows Media Video, is another major video format, the cousin to Microsoft's Windows Media Audio format. WMV, unlike AVI, is compressed. Numerous digital camcorders make use of WMV by default, so it is quite common. As you might expect, Ubuntu does not support the WMV format without the Restricted Extras package.

Another major format is the MP4 format, and is perhaps the most widely used format of the ones we will discuss here. A variant version of MP4 is the default format of Apple's QuickTime software (known as MOV files), and due to the Macintosh's popularity with video editing, MP4 files are quite common. MP4 does not work on Ubuntu without the Restricted Extras package.

You have probably noticed a repetitive theme here – Ubuntu generally does not support many media formats by default. Why not? As we discussed in the Introduction to this book, Canonical tries to uphold the principles of free software – which means not including proprietary or closed-source software. However, since this so severely limits Ubuntu's utility, given how many people use multimedia files, why should anyone use Ubuntu?

Fortunately, there is a simple and easy way to enable restricted file formats on Ubuntu, which we shall discuss in the next section.

The Ubuntu Restricted Extras

The Ubuntu Restricted Extras are a collection of multimedia codecs that allow you to view and listen to proprietary media formats on your Ubuntu system. Ubuntu, due to Canonical's support for free software, generally does not include closed-source software with Ubuntu. Starting with Ubuntu 10.10 Maverick Meerkat, the Ubuntu installer included an option to install the MP3 codec (along with a few other codecs, such as the Adobe Flash pluging) during the installation process.

However, this option doesn't install all the restricted codecs. If you skipped that step during the installation, the Ubuntu Restricted Extras package is quite easy to install.

To do so, open up a Terminal window and type this command:

sudo apt-get install ubuntu-restricted-extras

Enter your password to authenticate, and apt-get will download and install the Ubuntu Restricted Extras packages for you. After the installation is complete, you should be able to play media in proprietary formats.

(Note that you should only install the Restricted Extras if it is legal to do so in your country of residence.)

Converting Audio With Sound Converter

If you have a WAV file that you want to convert to an MP3, it's possible to do so quite easily and simply on a Ubuntu system. You just need two software packages: the Ubuntu Restricted Extras packages, and the GNOME Sound Converter application. The Sound

Converter program offers a GUI for converting sound files from one format to another.

First, you'll need to install the Ubuntu Restricted Extras package, which we discussed in the previous section.

To install the Sound Converter program itself, go to a Terminal window and type this command:

sudo apt-get install soundconverter

After you enter your password to authenticate, apt-get will download and install SoundConverter and its necessary dependencies. After the installation is complete, you can launch Sound Convert by going to the Activities Overview, searching for "soundconverter", and clicking on the Sound Converter icon.

Once the program has launched, go to the Edit menu, and to the Options item. From there you can set the kind of output you want the program to produce (OGG files, MP3 files, or AAC files), as well as the destination folder for the converted files. Once you've selected your preferences, hit the Close button, and then Add Files on the program's main toolbar to choose the files you want to convert.

Convert Audio And Video With Ffmpeg

From time to time you may need to extract the sound from a video file. Fortunately, using the ffmpeg program, it's quite simple to take the sound from any video file and store it as a separate file. The ffmpeg utility can convert back and forth between multiple formats of both video and sound. Even better, in keeping with the overall theme of this book, ffmpeg is a command-line utility.

Here's how to install and use ffmpeg on Ubuntu.

First, you'll need to install the Ubuntu Restricted Extras package so ffmpeg can effectively move files between formats, which we described how to do earlier in this chapter.

After you've installed the Ubuntu Restricted Extras, use this command to install ffmpeg:

sudo apt-get install ffmpeg

After the installation is complete, you can use ffmpeg to extract the audio from a video file. Say, for example, you have a video file named test.avi. To extract the audio to a file named audio.mp3, use ffmpeg with these options and arguments:

ffmpeg -i test.avi audio.mp3

This will create an audio file named audio.mp3 containing the sound from the video file. However, by default ffmpeg creates audio files with a bitrate of 64 kbps, which results in very low-quality audio. To force ffmpeg to create the mp3 file at the 256 kbps bitrate, add the -ab option to the command:

ffmpeg -i test.avi -ab 256k audio.mp3

This will create a higher-quality mp3 file, and you can use this modified command to extract the audio from any compatible video file.

The ffmpeg utility can do many other conversions as well – be sure to read the entire manual page for ffmpeg with this command:

man ffmpeg

Convert Video With Handbrake

The popular Handbrake application is designed to convert DVD video into a format that portable media players can use, and can also do some video format conversion as well. Best of all, the installation only takes a few Terminal commands.

(Note that since Handbrake tends not to work on new versions of Ubuntu without an update, these directions may become out of date with the next version of Ubuntu.)

Go to a Terminal window and type this command:

sudo apt-get install handbrake

After the installation is complete, you can launch Handbrake by going to the Activities Overview, searching for "Handbrake", and clicking on the program's icon.

View Media With Vlc

(We already discussed installing VLC Media Player in Chapter 14, but it seems appropriate to repeat the information here.)

VLC Media Player is a handy program that can play numerous forms of video, and runs on just about any OS platform. It also runs on Ubuntu, and installing it is quite simple.

First, open up a Terminal window and type this command:

sudo apt-get install vlc

Enter your password to authenticate, and apt will download and install VLC and its various dependencies for you. (You can also install it through Synaptic Package Manager and Ubuntu Software Center.) Afterwards you can launch VLC by going to the Dash, searching for "VLC", and clicking on the VLC icon.

Of course, most of the media you watch will probably be found on the Internet, which means you'll want the VLC plugins for Firefox. Fortunately, the VLC Firefox plug is also easy to install. Return to the Terminal and type this command:

sudo apt-get install vlc vlc-plugin-* mozilla-plugin-vlc

Once you enter your password, apt-get will install the Firefox VLC plugin. You can check that the plugin is installed by going to Firefox, to the Tools menu, and selecting Add-ons. Once in the Add-ons dialog box, you can view all your plugins by hitting the Plugins button. You should see the VLC plugins listed there.

Of course, VLC needs codecs into order to display certain kinds of video. You may need to install the Ubuntu Restricted Extras package in order to get maximum use out of VLC.

20

CONFIGURING UBUNTU UNITY

A s of Ubuntu 11.04 Natty Narwhal, Canonical introduced a new user interface for Ubuntu called "Unity." Previously part of Ubuntu Netbook Edition (which was discontinued when Unity became the interface for the desktop edition of Ubuntu), Unity offers a radical change in the user interface from previous versions of Ubuntu. In this chapter, we will take a look at Unity and how to change some of its settings.

As of April 2017, Canonical will no longer work on Unity, and Ubuntu 17.10 will return to using GNOME Shell. Ubuntu 18.04 is the first long-term support release to use GNOME Shell instead of Unity.

What Is Unity?

Technically, Unity is a shell interface running on top of the GNOME Desktop Environment. A desktop environment is the set of programs and settings that create the graphical desktop, and most desktop Linux distributions use one of two major desktop environments: GNOME and KDE. (There are of course many others.) Unity, there-fore, is a shell running on top of GNOME, a shell designed to make more efficient use of the available screen space.

The most visually obvious change about Unity is the Launcher, the dock-like toolbar running the height of the left side of the screen. The icons for running applications appear in the Launcher, with a little triangle on the left side of the icon to indicate that they are running. You can also pin frequently-used applications to the Launcher by right-clicking them and selecting "Keep in Launcher."

The second most obvious UI change in Unity is the button with the Ubuntu logo at the top of the Launcher. Clicking on the Ubuntu button will bring up the Dash, an integrated system-wide search application. Typing in the Dash's search box will search your entire system for applications, files, and folders. For instance, if you wanted to launch the Google Chrome web browser, you will type in "chrome", and the Dash would bring up the icon for Chrome (which you could then pin to the Launcher).

The Dash also has a number of "lenses", which lets you view all items in a specific category. For instance, you can view all applications, or files and folders. You can also see your most frequently used applications.

Canonical, Ubuntu's parent company, had a grand vision of creating a single interface that could run on desktops, laptops, tablets, and mobile phones. However, this vision proved too ambitious, and in April 2017, Canonical announced it was shutting down the Unity project and switching back to GNOME Shell for future versions of Ubuntu. However, Ubuntu 16.04 Xenial Xerius will receive support until 2021, so Unity isn't finished quite yet.

Considering the radical changes in the UI, it is not all surprising that Unity provoked a very strong response in the Ubuntu community – people seem to either love it or hate it. However, it is possible to adjust the settings on Unity somewhat to create a UI experience more to your taste, which we will discuss in the next section.

Unity Settings Prior To 12.04

Versions of Ubuntu prior to 12.04 do not include any way to alter the settings or performance of Unity. Which is rather strange – Windows

7 lets you alter the Taskbar a great deal, and Mac OS X permits a considerable amount of customization for its Dock. However, Unity runs off a piece of software called Compiz, which is the window manager – the program that actually draws and moves the windows on your desktop. Using Compiz's configuration program, called CompizConfig Settings Manager, you can adjust some of Unity's settings.

Here's how to install it.

Go to a Terminal window and enter this command:

sudo apt-get install compizconfig-settings-manager

Enter your password to authenticate, and apt will download and install the CompizConfig Settings Manager for you. After the installation is complete, you can launch the CompizConfig Settings Manager by going to the Dash, searching for "compiz", and click on the icon for CompizConfig Settings Manager. You can also launch it by going to the Terminal and typing this command:

ccsm

Once the Settings Manager program launches, scroll down to the Desktop category, and click on the Ubuntu Unity plugin.

You can then adjust some of Unity's settings from here. There are two main tabs: Behaviour, and Experimental.

The Behaviour tab lets you edit the keys to control Unity. Specifically, you can change the key to show the Launcher (by default, the "Super" key, which on most PCs is the key with the Windows logo between the CTRL and ALT keys). You can also edit the key to put the keyboard focus on the Launcher, the keystroke to run a command, and the key to open the first panel menu.

The Experimental tab lets you change the Launcher's graphical behavior. The most useful setting here is the Launcher Icon Size slider. Adjusting this to the left or right changes the size of the Launcher icons. This lets you reduce the amount of screen space the Launcher uses, which is quite useful on a smaller display.

Once you have finished making changes, you will have to restart your Ubuntu system for the changes to take effect.

Unfortunately, it is not currently possible to move the Launcher to the bottom of the screen, like the Mac OS X dock, or to the right.

Unity 2D Prior To 12.04

Unity offers a great deal of graphical eye candy, but unfortunately that eye candy requires a graphics card with a least a reasonable level of power to support it. This means that older computers often cannot run the Unity interface. Fortunately, Ubuntu includes a fallback option - Unity 2D. Unity 2D doesn't have all the bells and whistles, but it will let you use Unity on a system that might not have the graphical chops to support the full version.

Here's how to use it.

At the logon screen, click on the gear icon next to your username. In the dropdown menu, you'll see the different desktop environments available for your Ubuntu system. Select "Ubuntu 2D" and log in.

You will then use Unity 2D for your desktop environment.

(If you hate Unity entirely, GNOME and GNOME Classic are both available for you to use, and as of Ubuntu 17.10, Unity has been discontinued.)

CHANGE UNITY SETTINGS IN UBUNTU 12.04 AND LATER VERSIONS

UBUNTU DOES NOT LET you change very many settings with the Launcher. You can rearrange the Launcher's icons, but you cannot disable the Launcher entirely, or configure it to appear on the bottom or right side of the screen, the way Mac users can with the Dock in OS X. However, you can quite easily adjust the size of the Launcher. If you have a small screen, making the Launcher smaller reduces the amount of screen space it occupies. As an added bonus, you can then pin more icons to the Launcher.

To change the Launcher's size, first launch the System Settings application. The System Settings application is pinned to the Launcher by default, and the icon looks like a wrench superimposed over a gear.

After the System Settings application launches, click on the Appearance icon, which is the first icon on the top row of icons.

When the Appearance category opens, you will see a scroll bar that says "Launcher icon size" at the bottom of the window.

You can then adjust the size of the Launcher by dragging the indicator on the scroll bar back and forth. The larger the number, the larger the Launcher and its icons will be. You can play with the setting until you find one that fits your screen comfortably.

You can also configure the Launcher to hide itself automaticaly unless you move the mouse o the Launcher's designated "hot spot". To enable this setting, click on the Behavior tab and set the "Auto-hide the Launcher" option to On.

Unity Tweak Tool

Ubuntu's Unity is very useful, but it's not very configurable. You can change whether or not the Dash searches online sources, or the size of the Launcher, but that's essentially it. However, you can use the third-party Unity Tweak Tool to further customize the behavior and attributes of the Dash, the Launcher, and other aspects of Unity.

First, you'll need to install Unity Tweak Tool. You can do so by going to the Ubuntu Software application (pinned to the Launcher by default), searching for "Unity Tweak Tool", and install it from there. If you prefer the Terminal, you can install Unity Tweak Tool with this command:

sudo apt-get install unity-tweak-tool

After the installation, you can launch Unity Tweak Tool by going to the Dash, searching for "Unity", and clicking on the icon for Unity Tweak Tool. After Unity Tweak Tool launches, go to the Unity category, and then click on the icon for Search.

You will then see a number of additional options for the Dash under the Search category. You can adjust whether or not the Dash will blur the background when it appears. You can also control whether or not the Dash will search online sources (similar to the option in System Settings).

Under the Applications heading, you can adjust whether or not the Dash will show "more suggestions" when you search for an applications, and whether or not it will list Recently Used applications. Under the Files heading, you can control whether or not the Dash is able to search your files. Disable this setting, and the Dash will not search your files.

Finally, under the Run Command heading, clicking the Clear History button will purge your history of Dash searches. Clicking the Restore Defaults button will reset the Dash to its default settings.

You will then see a number of additional options for the Launcher. You can set it to "auto-hide", meaning it will disappear unless you move the mouse to the left side of the screen to summon it back. Additionally, you can adjust the color and transparency of the Launcher. By default, the Launcher derives its color from your desktop wallpaper, but if you would prefer it to look different, you can adjust that setting here.

Finally, you can also alter the Launcher's animation settings under the "Icons" heading. You can adjust the size of the Icons, like in System Preferences, but you can also customize the animations icons use when launching an application or presenting a notification. One useful switch here is the "Show Desktop" setting, which lets you pin a button to immediately show the desktop to the bottom of the Launcher.

If you dislike the changed settings, you can restore the defaults at any time by clicking on the "Restore defaults" button.

Additional Notes

For a fuller explanation of Ubuntu Unity, check out my book The Ubuntu Desktop Beginner's Guide, which is devoted to the Ubuntu graphical interface.

21

GNOME SHELL

Since 2011, Ubuntu has by default used the Unity desktop environment as its default interface. Unity was part of a grand vision of convergence, the idea that you could take a Ubuntu phone, plug it into a dock, and use it as a desktop computer. Unfortunately, the idea proved a little too ambitious, and in 2017, Canonical announced that Unity was canceled, and starting with Ubuntu 17.10 Artful Aardvark, the Ubuntu desktop would henceforth use a customized version of GNOME Shell.

In this chapter, we'll show you how to use and customize GNOME Shell on Ubuntu Linux.

Customize The Ubuntu Dock

The Dock is the successor to the Launcher in the Unity desktop, and it serves much the same purpose. The Dock displays running applications and offers a shortcut to the Application View screen, which lets you view all the applications installed on your Ubuntu system. In the Unity desktop, the Launcher was locked to the left-hand side of the screen. In GNOME Shell, you can set the Dock to display on the left-hand side of the screen, the right-hand side of the screen, or the bottom of the screen (similar to the position of the Dock in MacOS on Apple Macintosh computers). Additionally, you can also adjust the size of icons on the Dock, which is useful if you are running Ubuntu on a smaller screen with lower resolution.

To change the position of the Dock, click on the Application View button on the bottom of the Dock. When the Application View appears, launch the System Settings application. When the System Settings application opens, click on the Dock item in the left-hand pane. The right-hand pane of the window will then display the settings options for the Dock.

To change the Dock's placement on the screen, adjust the drop-down menu labeled Position On The Screen. You can select Left, Right, and Bottom, and the Dock will immediately move to that position on the screen.

You can also change the size of the icons on the Dock by dragging the Icon Size slider. The smaller you make the Dock, the more icons you can fit on it, but it will be harder to see. The default size for the Dock is 48, if you decide you prefer the original size.

Pin And Unpin Applications

The Ubuntu Dock is the successor to the Launcher in the old Unity desktop, and the Launcher allowed you to lock application icons to it. That way you could quickly run those applications by clicking on its icon on the Launcher. The Ubuntu Dock uses a similar system. The items locked to the Dock are called Favorites, and you can pin and unpin an application to the Dock with ease.

To pin an application to the Dock, first click on the Application View button at the bottom of the Dock. This will bring up a list of every application installed on your Ubuntu system. Scroll through the icons until you find the application you want, and then right-click on it and select Add To Favorites. The application's icon will then be added to your Dock.

You can rearrange the order of the Favorites on your Dock by left-clicking on the icon in the Dock and then holding down the mouse button. That will allow you to drag the icon to a new position on the Dock.

To remove an icon from the Dock, right-click on it and select Remove From Favorites. The icon will then be removed from the Dock.

Ubuntu Dock Keyboard Shortcuts

Typically, you use the Dock in Ubuntu to launch applications by clicking on the individual icons for the applications. However, the Dock has a useful shortcut that allows you to launch applications from the keyboard.

By default in a new installation of Ubuntu, Firefox is pinned at the first location on the Dock, Rhythmbox Music Player at the second, and Nautilus File Explorer at the third location. By holding down the SUPER key (usually the WINDOWS key on most PC keyboards) and a number key, you can launch an application in the order is is pinned to the dock. For example, with a default dock, hitting SUPER+1 would launch Firefox, hitting SUPER+2 would launch Rhythmbox, and hitting SUPER+3 would launch Nautilus.

If you wanted to launch a second instance of an already-running application, add the SHIFT key to the mix. For example, to open a second instant of Firefox, hit SUPER+SHIFT+1, and a new Firefox window will open.

Finally, if you want to check which numeric keys correspond to which application icons on the Dock, simply hold down the SUPER key. The appropriate number will appear atop each icon on the Dock.

Activities Overview

The Activities Overview is a useful aspect of GNOME Shell that lets you both search for installed applications or view running applications.

To use Activities Overview, click on the Activities button in the upper left-hand corner of the screen. The desktop view will be replaced with the Activities search box in the top half of the screen and miniature windows showing the running applications on your system in the bottom half of the screen. You can also get to the Activities Overview by hitting the SUPER key on your keyboard.

To search for applications, simply start typing in the search box in the top half of the screen. Activities Overview will then find the applications that match your search term.

To switch to a running application, simply click on its miniaturized window in the bottom half of the screen. Ubuntu will immediately exit out of Activities Overview and take you to that application. You can also use Activities Overview to close any running applications. Just hover the mouse pointer over one of the running applications. The application window in question will be surrounded with an orange border, with a black X in the upper right-hand corner. Click on the black X, and the application will be closed.

Gnome Tweak Tool

The System Settings application lets you change the size and the position of the Dock, but if you want to customize the desktop environment further, you will need to use the GNOME Tweak Tool. This utility lets you customize many aspects of GNOME Shell, and it works in Ubuntu.

To install the GNOME Tweak Tool, go to a Terminal window and type this command:

sudo apt-get install gnome-tweak-tool

Enter your password to authenticate, and Ubuntu will install the GNOME Tweak Tool for you. After the installation is complete, you can launch GNOME Tweak Tool by going to the Activities Overview, typing "tweak" into the search box, and clicking on the icon for GNOME Tweak Tool.

Once GNOME Tweak Tool launches, in the left-hand pane of the window you will see ten different categories for configuring GNOME Shell.

Appearance lets you adjust the theme, the animations, and the appearance of the cursors and the icons.

The Desktop category lets you set whether or not icons will appear on the Desktop, and allows you to customize the wallpaper image and the lock screen image.

The Extension category lets you turn on and off any installed extensions for GNOME Shell.

The Fonts category controls which fonts GNOME Shell uses, as well as their size.

The Keyboard & Mouse category allows you adjust settings for the behavior of the keyboard and mouse. If you are using Ubuntu on a laptop computer and want the touchpad to automatically disable itself while you are typing, this setting is found here.

The Power category controls whether or not a laptop computer sleeps when the lid is closed.

The Startup Applications category allows you to configure which applications are permitted to start automatically when you log into a Ubuntu session.

The Top Bar category controls the behavior of the bar running alone the top of the screen in a GNOME Shell session. You can set whether or not the laptop battery percentage, the clock, and the calendar are visible in the top bar.

The Windows category controls the behavior of windows in GNOME Shell. You can adjust how windows maximize and mini-mize, how windows work with focus, and what happens when you double-click on the title bar.

Finally, the Workspaces category configures how Ubuntu handles "Workspaces", which is what it calls virtual desktops.

Install Extensions

Ubuntu now uses GNOME Shell, and one of the nice things about GNOME shell is that it is infinitely customization through exten-sions. It takes a bit of work to install extensions for GNOME Shell in Ubuntu, but once it is finished, you can install extensions at will.

To install extensions in GNOME Shell, you have to use a web browser, and you can use either Firefox or Chrome for that purpose. If you wish to use Firefox to install GNOME Shell extensions, open Firefox, visit this web page, and install the GNOME Shell Integration plugin for Firefox:

https://addons.mozilla.org/en-US/firefox/addon/gnome-shell-integration/

If you wish to use Chrome to install GNOME Shell extensions, open Chrome, and then visit this web page to install the GNOME Shell Integration plugin for Chrome:

https://chrome.google.com/webstore/detail/gnome-shell-integration/gphhapmejobijbbhgpjhcjognlahblep

Once that is finished, open a Terminal window by hitting the CTRL+ALT+T keys simultaneously, and then type this command:

sudo apt-get install chrome-gnome-shell

(Note that both Firefox and Chrome use the chrome-gnome-shell package.)

Once chrome-gnome-shell has finished installing, close your web browser and launch it again, and then navigate to this web page:

https://extensions.gnome.org

The most popular extensions will be listed. Click on each extension, and you will see a graphical ON/OFF slider switch. To install an extension, simply slide the extension's switch to the ON position. A pop-up menu will ask if you wish to install the extension, and click on the INSTALL button to continue. To uninstall an installed extension, move the slider back to the OFF position.

22

MANAGING PROCESSES

W e've already discussed process management a bit in CHAPTER 5 – MONITORING MEMORY AND DISK SPACE USAGE. However, monitoring processes – both keeping track of their resource usage and terminating them when necessary – is an important part of Ubuntu Linux system administration. In this chapter we will discuss process management from the command line in more detail.

What Is A Process?

Technically speaking, a process is active instance of a computer program. So all the programs and applications you run on your Ubuntu machine are processes. For instance, if you were to run the Firefox web browser, and then execute the top command, you'll see the "firefox" process displayed in the list of running process. When you exit the program, that process will exit and disappear. (Unless something goes wrong, which will discuss more with the section on the kill command.)

Processes are sometimes referred to as "daemons", but the two terms aren't identical. A daemon is in fact a process. However, the term "daemon" usually refers to a system process running in the background. The SSH daemon is one such background system process – it waits until it hears as SSH request over the network connection, regardless of what any standard users are currently doing on the system. Generally, system daemons have a "d" at the end of their names (the SSH daemon is named "sshd") to distinguish them from processes that you or other users might have launched on the system.

First, we'll discuss how to view currently running processes with the ps command.

The Ps Command

Needless to say, administering your system requires you to keep a close eye on running processes. There are any number of commands and utilities for monitoring your system's processes, but one of the simplest is the venerable ps command. To use the ps command, simply type it at the command prompt:

ps

However, without any switches, ps is not terribly useful. The default output without any switches looks like this:

```
PID TTY          TIME CMD
2589 pts/1    00:00:00 bash
4366 pts/1    00:00:00 ps
```

In its default state, ps only shows the currently running process – itself – and the shell you are currently using. Fortunately, you can make ps much more useful with the –e switch:

ps –e

The –e stands for Extended, and generates a listing of every process currently running on the system.

```
PID TTY          TIME CMD
  1 ?        00:00:00 init
  2 ?        00:00:00 kthreadd
  3 ?        00:00:03 ksoftirqd/0
  5 ?        00:00:00 kworker/u:0
  6 ?        00:00:00 migration/0
  7 ?        00:00:00 cpuset
  8 ?        00:00:00 khelper
```

However, this still only displays a limited amount of information, especially when compared to the top command. You can tell the ps command to display more information with the –l switch:

ps -el

The –l switch stands for Long Listing, and generates quite a bit more information. Specifically, you can see the UID (user ID) of the user who launched the process, the PPID (parent PID) of the parent process of a child process, the process's priority and nice, and numerous other useful pieces of information. For even more information, use ps with the –f switch:

ps –elf

In addition to the information offered by the –l switch, the addition of the –f switch also causes the ps command to display the date the process was launched and the location of its executable on the file system.

Even ps –elf is only a static snapshot of the processes currently running on the system. The running processes can change very quickly on a Linux system, and you might want to monitor them in real-time. That's where the top command comes in.

The Top Command

The top command has been around forever, and is included in practically every variant of Linux. Ubuntu is no exception. The top command displays a variety of useful statistics, including the "top" users of CPU time (hence the command's name), the amount of memory running processes are using, the amount of virtual memory they are using, the process's priority, the process's owning user, and numerous other useful pieces of information. To launch top, simply type the command at the command prompt:

top

Once launched, top stays running, displaying statistics in real time. Processes are listed by their process ID number, along the name of the command that started the process.

There's a lot of information listed in top, so let's take a look at the available statistics:

PID: A process's process ID number.

USER: The process's owner. Processes owned by root are usually system processes, and should be left alone unless they cause problems.

PR: The process's priority, which determines how much attention the CPU will give this process over other processes. The lower the number, the higher the priority.

NI: The nice value of the process, which affects its priority.

VIRT: How much virtual memory the process is using.

RES: How much physical RAM the process is using, measured in kilobytes.

SHR: How much shared memory the process is using.

S: The current status of the process (zombied, sleeping, running, uninterruptedly sleeping, or traced).

%CPU: The percentage of the processor time used by the process.

%MEM: The percentage of physical RAM used by the process.

TIME+: How much processor time the process has used.

COMMAND: The name of the command that started the process.

Of course, you may want to sort the top display by a certain category from least to greatest. This is especially useful when you want to figure out what process is hogging the most CPU time or memory. Hitting the 't' key will sort the processes by CPU time. Hitting 'l' will sort by load average, and 'm' by memory info.

Like the GNOME System Monitor application, you can also use top to kill uncooperative processes. To do this, you'll need to make note of the process ID you want to kill. Hit the "k" key while top is running, and the utility will ask you to input a process ID number.

Input the number, hit Enter, and then hit Enter again when it asks if you want to kill the process (top assumes you mean "yes" when you hit enter). The top utility will then kill the process.

Once you've finished with top, hit the q key to exit and return to the command line.

Most often, you'll use the top and ps commands to track down process that's causing trouble. In the next section, we'll discuss how to terminate troublesome processes with the (appropriately named) kill command.

The Kill Command

The kill command, as you might guess from the name, lets you kill running processes.

Technically, the kill command sends signals to running processes. However, this command is most commonly used to send the kill a running process. In most cases, you will use this command to terminate a process that has frozen up, refuses to quit gracefully, or is otherwise misbehaving. Using kill, you can terminate troublesome processes.

Note that to use kill, you need to know the PID (process identification number) of the process you wish to terminate. You can find out the PID using either the ps or the top commands (detailed elsewhere in this book).

To use kill, simply type the command with the PID of the targeted process. For instance, to terminate a process with the PID of 2589:

kill 2589

Like other commands, kill can be modified with a number of switches. Remember that kill operates by sending signals to the designated process. The kill command uses 64 separate signals, which you can list with the –l switch:

kill –l

Of those 64 signals, four of them are commonly used. You tell kill which signal to send by using the signal's number as a switch – for instance, kill- 9 2589.

15 is the default kill signal. 15 tells the targeted process to cease immediately, but only after shutting down gracefully. Since 15 is the default kill signal, you don't usually have explicity specify it, but if you did, the command to send the 15 signal to PID 2589 would look like this:

kill -15 2589

Signal number 1 less drastic. It merely tells the process to restart, while keeping the same PID. To use signal number 1:

kill -1 2589

Signal number 2 sends the CTRL+C character combination to a process, which is commonly used to break out of a running process (the ping command, for instance). To send signal number 2 to a process:

kill -2 2589

Finally, the most drastic signal is number 9. Signal number 9 immediately kills a process, and does not give it the option to close gracefully or clean up after itself first. Generally, you should only use signal number 9 to terminate a process if nothing else has worked first:

kill -9 2589

Using ps, top, and kill, you can manage the running processes on your Ubuntu system from the command line, and quickly respond to any problems.

23

WORKING WITH DOCUMENTS FROM THE COMMAND LINE

W hen working with "documents" (such as spreadsheets, presentations, PDF files, text documents, and the like), you will spend most of your time in Ubuntu's graphical interface since most of the tools for working with documents are in the GUI. If you need to create an elaborate document or a complex spreadsheet, you will need to use a program in the GUI. (I suppose you could write a novel in the vi text editor, but it probably would not be a pleasant experience.)

That said, there are several command line utilities that allow you to automate certain document management tasks. For example, let's say you have forty PDF files you need to merge into a single PDF document, or three hundred ODT documents you need to convert to HTML files. If you perform these tasks in the GUI, it will take a great deal of repetitive, tedious, and time-consuming pointing and clicking with the mouse. However, with a few well-chosen commands, you can easily handle several tedious document-management tasks.

Manage Pdf Files With Pdftk

PDF stands for Portable Document Format, and has become the de facto standard for official government documents and corporate documents – think of how many times you have had to visit a government website or your employer's website to download and fill out an official form in PDF. The upside to this is that a document creator can arrange to have a PDF look exactly the way he wants it, since PDFs are readable on many different operating systems and devices. The downside is that if you need to change a PDF file after it has been created, changing it is both annoying and difficult.

The is where the pdftk utility comes into play. The pdftk utility (it's short for "PDF Toolkit") allows you to combine and separate PDF files. It's not included in the default installation of Ubuntu, but you can rectify that in short order from the command line. Log into an account with administrative rights, go to a Terminal window, and type this command:

sudo apt-get install pdftk

Enter your password to authenticate, and apt will download and install pdftk for you. After the installation is complete, you can use pdftk from the command line.

Now that you have pdftk installed, we'll show you how to use it combine PDF files. Let's say, for example, that you have three PDF files: Page1.pdf, Page2.pdf, and Page3.pdf. You need to combine them into a single PDF document called FinalDraft.pdf. You could do this via LibreOffice or another document editing program. Or you could do it with pdftk:

pdftk Page1.pdf Page2.pdf Page3.pdf output FinalDraft.pdf

This command will take the three PDF files and combine them into a single PDF named FinalDraft.pdf. Note that pdftk will combine the files in the order they are listed. So if you wanted Page3.pdf to actually be the first page in FinalDraft.pdf instead of Page1.pdf, you would use this command:

pdftk Page3.pdf Page2.pdf Page1.pdf output FinalDraft.pdf

This will create the FinalDraft.pdf document with the Page3.pdf as its first page.

You can also use pdftk to extract single pages from larger PDF documents. In this example, let's say you have a 90-page PDF document named Report.pdf. You want to extract only page 9 from this document so you can email it to a coworker. To extract page 9 from Report.pdf and save it as its own PDF document named Page9.pdf, use pdftk with these options:

pdftk A=Report.pdf cat A9 output Page9.pdf

This will take the ninth page from Report.pdf and save it as its own PDF document named Page9.pdf.

Likewise, you can also use pdftk to extract a range of pages from a PDF document and save them in their own file. To return to our previous example, if you wanted to extract pages 19 through 37 of Report.pdf in their own file named Extract.pdf, you would use pdftk with these options:

pdftk A=Report.pdf cat A19-37 output Extract.pdf

With pdftk, you can disassemble and reassemble PDF documents with ease.

Converting File Types With Libreoffice

LibreOffice, the free office suite included with Ubuntu, has a fairly useful feature that's not very well known. Called "headless mode", this allows you to run LibreOffice from the command line without launching any graphical interface components. Since LibreOffice is a full-featured office suite, this might seem like a waste of time. However, you can use LibreOffice's headless mode to perform batch conversions of files. Using it to convert, say, one *.doc file to a PDF document might seem cumbersome. However, if you have 2,000 *.doc files you need to convert to PDFs (as part of, to cite a common example, government regulatory compliance), this can save a tremendous amount of time.

In our first example, let's say you have 1,000 *.doc files you need to convert to PDFs. The document files are located in a directory called "source" in your home directory, and you want to have the PDFs in a directory called "output" in your home directory. The command to convert the doc files to PDF files will look like this:

libreoffice –headless –convert-to pdf:writer_pdf_Export -outdir ~/output ~/source/*.doc

This will take every single *.doc file in the ~/source directory and convert it to a corresponding PDF file in the ~/source directory. Note that the original *.doc files are not altered in any way.

You can also use this command to perform mass conversions of other file formats. For instance, let's say you wanted to turn those 1,000 *.doc files into HTML files instead. The command would look like this:

libreoffice –headless –convert-to html -outdir ~/output ~/source/*.doc

This will convert the *.doc files in ~/output to HTML files in ~/source. Again, the original document files will not be altered.

By changing the parameter after the –convert-to option, you can convert to and from any of the file types supported by LibreOffice. If you wanted to change your *.doc files in ~/source to *.odt files (Ope-Document Format files), the command would look like this:

libreoffice –headless –convert-to odt -outdir ~/output ~/source/*.doc

Using LibreOffice's command-line utility allows you to quickly and easily perform batch conversions of documents.

24

VNC CLIENT AND SERVER

I n this chapter, we're going to explain how to use your Ubuntu machine both as a VNC server and as a client. VNC is an extremely useful networking protocol that allows you to remotely control a machine as if you were sitting in front of it and using its keyboard and mouse. We'll show you how to configure your Ubuntu machine as a VNC server, and how to use Ubuntu to connect to other computers acting as VNC servers.

What Is Vnc?

The acronym "VNC" stands for "Virtual Network Computing", and allows a computer with a VNC server to transmit its keyboard, mouse, and monitor information to a remote computer. This essentially allows the remote computer to control the server computer. VNC technology was originally developed by the Oracle corporation in the 1990s, and the technology was later purchased by AT&T. A variety of different VNC implementations have been developed for every operating system, and this means a VNC client on, say, a Windows computer can control a VNC server on a Ubuntu system.

Security Limitations

Note that by default, the version of VNC included with Ubuntu does not encrypt the connection, so that means anyone listening in on your network can in theory see everything you do on the remote computer. So it's best only to use Ubuntu's VNC implementation on a local network, and on a computer that does not have high security needs.

With those limitations in mind, let's discuss how to set up Ubuntu as a VNC server.

Vnc Server

To access Ubuntu's VNC server capabilities, click on the Dash (the Ubuntu icon in the upper left-hand corner of your screen) and type "Desktop Sharing" into the search box:

Click on the icon, and Desktop Sharing, the utility that controls Ubuntu's VNC server, will then launch:

The Desktop Sharing utility offers a variety of options to customize the security and operating of Ubuntu's VNC server. We'll go through these options one by one.

The first option, "Allow other users to view your desktop", allows other users to view your desktop via a VNC client. However, in order to actual control your desktop, you need to check the "Allow other users to control your desktop" checkbox. Allowing other users to view, but not control, your desktop is useful in situations where you want other people to view your desktop without having the ability to affect your computer. For example, if you are running a presentation off your Ubuntu computer, this would allow you to share the presentation without letting the other users control your computer.

The next three options deal with security. The first, "You must confirm each access to this machine", means that every time someone tries to connect to your Ubuntu machine via VNC, you'll get a little pop-up box that looks like this:

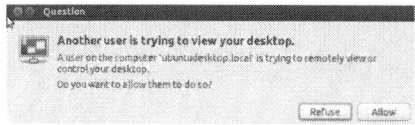

This allows you to refuse or allow VNC connections to your computer.

The next option lets you set an additional password to grant access to your computer via VNC. This adds an additional layer of security to your computer, since you can grant VNC access only to users to whom you have given the VNC password. Additionally, if you decide to revoke VNC access to your machine, you can do so by the simple method of changing your VNC password.

The final option, "Automatically configure UpnP router to open and forward ports", lets you configure the VNC server to accept connection from the Internet. Generally, it is only a good idea to do this only if you know exactly what you are doing, since it is a security risk. You will also have to configure your router to allow connections on the VNC ports.

Finally, the set of options in the "Show Notification Area Icon" category govern whether or not Ubuntu will display a notification icon when there is an active VNC connection. The icon looks like this:

You can set the icon to appear all the time in the notification area, allowing you quick access to the VNC settings, but generally the icon is most useful when it is set to appear when someone accesses your desktop.

Once you have selected the appropriate settings, you can save the settings by clicking on the Close button. The VNC server will run in the background, waiting for an incoming connection.

CONNECTING TO A UBUNTU VNC SERVER FROM ANOTHER UBUNTU MACHINE

NOTE that to connect to a VNC server, you will need to know the VNC server's IP address.

Ubuntu includes a useful remote-desktop client application called Remmina, which allows you to connect to a VNC server. Remmina is a useful program that can connect to a variety of different server types, but for now, we'll focus on using it to connect to a VNC server. To launch Remmina, go to the Dash, enter "remmina" into the search field, and click on the Remmina icon:

When Remmina launches, you'll see a window that looks like this:

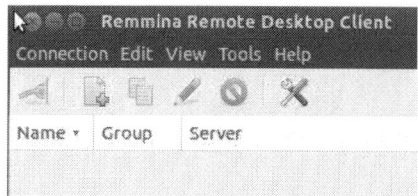

Click on the button with the green plus (+) sign to create a new connection. This will bring up the form for the new connection's details:

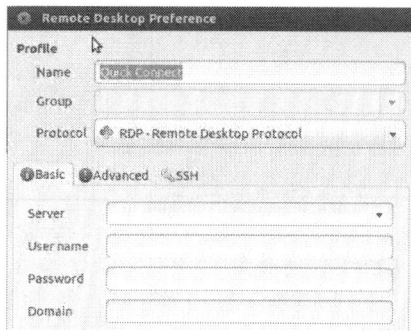

There are quite a few options here, but for a VNC connection, the main ones are the fields marked Protocol and Server. Change the Protocol drop-down menu to VNC:

Then enter the IP address of the VNC to which you wish to connect in the Server field. (Note that in this example, the VNC server must be on the same VLAN segment as your client computer.) Once you have entered the correct IP address, click on the Connect button at the bottom of the screen.

If the VNC Server was configured to require a password, you will then see a window like this:

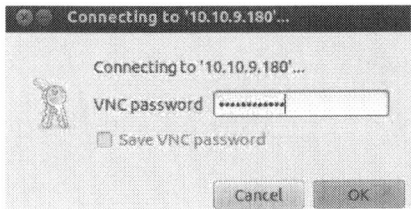

Enter the password, and you will be connected to the VNC server.

Forcibly Disconnecting A Vnc User

If a VNC client is connecting to your desktop and you want to forcibly disconnect it, click on the VNC icon in the notification area, and then select the Disconnect option:

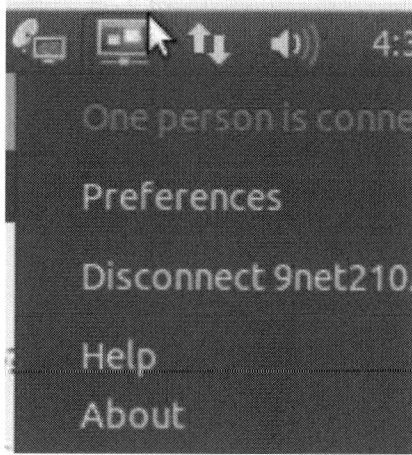

When you do, you'll see a dialog box asking if you want to discon-nect the remote user:

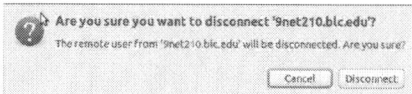

Click the Disconnect button, and the user will be disconnected.

AFTERWORD

I hope this book has been a useful introduction to Ubuntu Linux.

Ubuntu - and the entire technology world - changes very rapidly. Ubuntu's rapid release cycle means that a new version is available every six months, and other technological changes happen every day. Since this is an ebook, I hope to update it regularly to reflect the changes made in Ubuntu in particular and computing technology in general.

ABOUT THE AUTHOR

Standing over six feet tall, *USA Today* bestselling author Jonathan Moeller has the piercing blue eyes of a Conan of Cimmeria, the bronze-colored hair of a Visigothic warrior-king, and the stern visage of a captain of men, none of which are useful in his career as a computer repairman, alas.

He has written the DEMONSOULED series of sword-and-sorcery novels, and continues to write THE GHOSTS sequence about assassin and spy Caina Amalas, the COMPUTER BEGINNER'S GUIDE series of computer books, and numerous other works. His books have sold over three quarters of a million copies worldwide.

Visit his website at:

http://www.jonathanmoeller.com

Visit his technology blog at:

http://www.computerbeginnersguides.com

Made in the USA
Monee, IL
22 January 2020